OLD TESTAMENT

messianic prophecy

OLD TESTAMENT

messianic prophecy

AARON KLIGERMAN

ZONDERVAN PUBLISHING HOUSE
GRAND RAPIDS, MICHIGAN

INTRODUCTION

During the nineteenth century, the Christian Church was blessed with a number of great works on the Messianic prophecies of the Old Testament, by such scholars as Delitzsch, Hengstenberg, Kurtz, and Riehm, in Germany, and R. Payne Smith, David Baron, Edersheim, and Saphir, in England, the last three of whom were Christian Jews. In the twentieth century, however, at least until the last few years, the literature on Messianic prophecy, outside of strictly academic circles, has been very thin — ephemeral contributions which were but inadequate, disconnected collections of extracts from the writers of the preceding century, with expository comments of no particular importance.

As soon as I saw the first of a series of articles on Messianic prophecy by my friend Dr. Kligerman, appearing in the *Hebrew Christian Alliance Quarterly*, the thought came to me that here was a Christian Jew who could do a superb piece of work in this field, and that if he carried through his study with the same thoroughness that marked the initial article, the Christian Church should have access to this material in book form.

The author has done exactly what many of us hoped that he would do. From a life-long study of the Word of God, and a thorough acquaintance with post-Biblical Jewish literature, all of which has been tested through his many years as director of the Presbyterian Mission to the Jews in Baltimore, and other positions of equal importance, Dr. Kligerman has been able to give us the finest conservative study of Messianic prophecy, for the non-professional Bible student that has been published during the last thirty years.

Although I have been reading in this type of literature for years, I must say that a number of items in these pages are wholly new to me, e.g., his note on Genesis 3:15: "The Palestinian Targum testifies that in Genesis 3:15 there is promised a healing of the bite in the heel from the serpent, which is to take place 'at the end of the days, in the days of King Messiah.' In Bereshith rabba XII, the Midrash to Genesis, we read: 'The things which God created perfect since man sinned have become corrupt and do not return to their proper condition until the son of Perez (see Gen. 38:29, Ruth 4:18, the Messiah out of the tribe of Judah) comes.' According to this the Messiah is Saviour and Restorer." I immediately turned to see if there was any reference to these matters in Hershon's Talmudical Commentary on Genesis (London, 1883), only to discover that while this author devotes four pages to verse 14, and some lines to verse 16, there is no word on Genesis 3:15; likewise, the new *Soncino Chumash* (1947) contains no hint that this is a Messianic passage.

When our Lord was talking with the two disciples on the Emmaus road, that first Easter Sunday afternoon, we are told that "beginning from Moses and from all the prophets he interpreted to them in all the scriptures the things concerning himself" (Luke 24:27). Again, the same evening, He "opened their mind, that they might understand the scriptures; and said unto them, Thus it is written, that the Christ should suffer, and rise again from the dead the third day" (vv. 45, 46). It would be impossible to direct attention more emphatically to the pre-eminent importance of a knowledge of the Messianic prophecies than did our Lord in these post-resurrection utterances. We are told that as a result of our Lord's exegetical conversation, the disciples confessed, "Was not our heart burning within us, while he spake to us in the way, while he opened to us the scriptures?" May this be the experience — as well it may — of all who read these illuminating pages on this inexhaustible subject of Messianic prediction.

WILBUR M. SMITH

PREFACE

Amid the chaos and confusion of our modern world, there stands out the sure word of prophecy as a light shining in the darkness for our puzzled world to heed. The Bible from Genesis to Revelation is the revelation of Israel's Messiah, "the desire of all nations" (Hag. 2:7), the Saviour of the world. "All the prophets," our rabbis used to say, "prophesied only unto the days of the Messiah" (Berach. 34b). "The world itself was created for the sake of the Messiah" (Shabb. 63a). Dr. Charles Augustus Briggs, a great Biblical scholar says:

"Messianic Prophecy is the most important of all themes, for it is the ideal of redemption given by the Creator to our race at the beginning of its history, and it ever abides as the goal of humanity until the Divine plan has been accomplished."

In 1909 in the city of Odessa, Russia, when a Hebrew Christian minister of the Gospel laid before me God's plan of Salvation as revealed in the Messianic prophecies of the Old Testament, it made a profound impression and started me on the road to further investigate the claims of Jesus of Nazareth. This in turn led me to accept Him as Israel's promised Messiah and my personal Saviour and Lord. Having learned since by personal experience the preciousness of these grand Old Testament prophecies, I have freely used them in ministering to others the truths connected with these foreshadowings of the person and work of the Lord Jesus Christ.

It is futile to attempt a confession of my debt to others. Through a lifetime one learns from so many that he becomes quite unable to untangle and trace the threads of his thinking to their original sources. We are each a part of all we have met. I feel greatly indebted to a number of Hebrew

Christians, such as David Baron, Adolph Saphir, Alfred Edersheim, Max I. Reich, E. Bender Samuel and many others. My debt to the work of other scholars is, I hope, sufficiently acknowledged in the course of the book. Special acknowledgments are due to Dr. Wilbur M. Smith, a friend of many years, who in the midst of a busy ministry, as professor at Fuller Seminary and the author of many important books, took the time to read my articles on Messianic prophecy in the American *Hebrew Christian* and suggested that they be published in book form.

May it please God to use this book for the refreshment of His people, to quicken their desires in them after Himself, and to lead each and all of us to a more prayerful and diligent study of His Word, in which His purposes of redeeming grace and glory are treasured in the person and work of Israel's promised Messiah, our Lord Jesus Christ.

AARON J. KLIGERMAN

CONTENTS

EDITOR'S NOTES

The Twentieth Century Christian has experienced one of the most baffling of all religious educations. He has experienced the lukewarm, intellectual approach to Christianity that emphasized broad-mindedness. Should a Christian be broad-minded about sin? NO! This type of Christian education is the most useful tool the devil has ever used to ruin men's souls. It allows the most pagan heresies to be taught in the church along with the teachings of Jesus. Plato, Aristotle, and Socrates are equated with Christ. This is broad-mindedness; and therefore, most Sunday school lessons sound more like philosophy classes on inner peace than on the strict instruction of Godly living, as found in the Old and New Testaments.

The most terrible of these so-called broad-minded philosophies of the Twentieth Century is the Super Man Philosophers of Nietzsche. Dr. Nietzsche was one of the truly great Christian philosophers of the late 1800's, but unfortunately as a part of his Christian philosophers privilege, he served as a volunteer nurse during the Franco-Prussian War. There most authorities feel, he contracted a venereal disease which completely ruined his mind and body. From that time on until he collapsed a babbling mad man and died in a mental institution, he wrote a religious philosophy of the Super Man, which is in complete conflict with the teaching of the Bible, especially those of Jesus as he stressed total dependency on God. Adolph Hitler was greatly attracted to this type of Super Man philosophy, and he adopted it for his government which plunged the entire world into total chaos. The Twentieth Century Christian Church is coming dangerously close to doing the same thing. This generation is doing what Saul did. He disobeyed God when he did not completely destroy the Amalekites. He saved the best of the worst for the altar of his Lord, and because he disobeyed, the Lord, destroyed him.

This generation does not believe in the divinity of Christ, because church people blandly state that it is not necessary to believe that Mary was a virgin. The communist used this broad-minded religious teaching to brain-wash the Christian prisoners of war during the Korean police action. They argued most skillfully that if Mary was not a virgin then Jesus belonged to a mortal man, and therefore he was not divine. The Church was not founded on truth; and so man has only to answer to man. Communism could then declare that there was no God; so man's only God was the State; or worse still the mad mind of Nietzsche could bring forth the God is Dead idea, and people would believe that.

Dr. Kligerman has successfully repudiated all these deadly heresies, by carefully showing how all God's promises about Jesus were fulfilled in the Old Testament. He carefully gives the date and history of each prophecy and in which book it is found. He even gives the exact root-word in difficult passages and compares it to other similar words in the Old Testament; so that the reader's faith will be perfectly strengthened.

JUNE S. WOOD

Chapter I

MESSIANIC PROPHECY IN THE TORAH
(The Five Books of Moses)

Man in his present state is not what God intended him to be. He is a sinner "groaning and travailing in pain together" with the whole creation (Rom. 8:22) and under a curse. How man and creation reached that state we are told in the third chapter of Genesis, where we are for the first time introduced to this promise: "And I will put enmity between thee and the woman, and between thy seed and her seed; it shall bruise thy head and thou shalt bruise his heel" (Gen. 3:15). This was the young world's hope and the root idea of which all others are but shoots and branches and fruit.

To get a clear understanding of the prophetic utterances of the Old Testament we must examine the attitude of the New Testament writers toward these Messianic prophecies. The New Testament is a trustworthy guide for a journey of investigation into the Old Testament for the following reasons:

A. It is in a position to give us the best view possible, since it was written out of a real experience and so near the Old Testament days.

B. Like a telescope, it brings these precious promises nearer to us, making their outline and atmosphere clearer and more real.

C. It claims to have the right of interpreting the Old Testament and time has justified this claim.

On examining the New Testament we are immediately face to face with some interesting facts. We discover:

1. That Jesus never accused the leaders of Jewry of adding to or taking away from the Scriptures. To be sure they were reproached with ignorance of Scriptures, and with making the Law void and of none effect by adding the traditions of the fathers (Matt. 15:6; Mark 7:13), but never of tampering with the text in any way.

2. That Jesus often recognizes Moses as legislator and writer (Matt. 19:8; Luke 16:31; 24:27; John 5:46,47).

3. That Jesus took the liberty of applying certain Scriptures to Himself. On His visit to the town of Nazareth He naturally visited the local synagogue. The elders of the synagogue noticing a visitor, invited Him up the Bima to take part in the reading of the Portion of the Week, a custom held among the Jews to this day. They gave him the Book and the Haftorah for that Sabbath must have been from Isaiah sixty-one. Following the reading of the lesson, with the eyes of the congregation on Him, He spoke these momentous words:

> The Spirit of the Lord is upon me, because he hath anointed me to preach the gospel to the poor; He hath sent me to heal the brokenhearted, to preach deliverance to the captives, and recovering of sight to the blind, to set at liberty them that are bruised, to preach the acceptable year of the Lord.

And as He closed the Book, He said, "This day is this scripture fulfilled in your ears" (Luke 4:16-21).

On another occasion, when John the Baptist, as Herod's prisoner, heard of Jesus' fame, he sent some of his followers to interview the Nazarene and ask Him, "Art thou he that should come, or look we for another?" (Matt. 11:3). Jesus answered them, "Go to John and tell him of the things you hear and see," reminding him of Isaiah 29:18; 35:4-6; 42:6, 7; 61:1; 66:2. Especially convincing are the words spoken by Jesus to the two He walked with on the way to Emmaus: "O foolish ones, and slow of heart to believe all that the prophets have spoken" (Luke 24:25; 13-34).

The apostles as writers and preachers for Christ made the same use of the Old Testament as did their Lord, applying all the Old Testament prophecies to Him who came, lived, died, and rose again, according to the Scriptures. (See Acts 2: 14-36; 3:12-26; 8:26-40; 13:32,33; 17:2, 3; 26:22, 23; Rev. 19: 10). These New Testament Jews are the best interpreters of the Old Testament prophets. They were the EYEWITNESSES of the coming of Him who was the "Hope of Israel," the "Desire of the Nations," and the only Saviour of the world.

In the first eight chapters of Genesis we find the brightest possible narrative of a long stretch of human life on earth. These chapters probably cover as many centuries as the remainder of the Old Testament. Here too we become acquainted with the hidden source of the bright hope which upheld Israel through many dark centuries, centuries of suffering and persecution.

The first prophecy began with a significant utterance in the form of a promise, called by Old Testament scholars —

I. PROTEVANGELIUM

The promise in Genesis 3:15, reads: "I will put enmity between thee and the woman, and between thy seed and her seed; it shall bruise thy head, and thou shalt bruise his heel."

Three things stand out in this early but significant prophecy, namely, that the Deliverer must be —

A. Of the *seed of the woman* and

B. That He is to be *temporarily hindered* and

C. *Finally victorious.*

The coming of the serpent had prevailed. Sin, sorrow, and death have become realities in human life. But the tempter was not left to gloat with impunity over the ruin he had caused. Nor did God leave His children to eternal defeat and despair. In the darkest hour of human history, God's promise of ultimate victory brought comfort and cheer. This, then, is the first Messianic promise, the promise of the utter destruction of the serpent who is responsible for the ruination of mankind.

That Satan was the actual tempter is admitted by both Jewish and Christian writers. Hence he is always called *hanachash hakkadmon*, "the ancient serpent." He is also called Smmael (see *Hebraica Horae* on John 8:44, Rev. 12: 7-9). In Wisdom 2:24, it is stated, "Through envy of the devil came death into the world." In Revelation 12:9, he is spoken of as "the great dragon, that old serpent, called the Devil and Satan." In John 8:44, Christ calls the Devil "a manslayer from the beginning," which refers, no doubt, to his tempting Eve, by which death came into the world.

Now, since Satan, the actual tempter, cannot be separated from the serpent, the instrument in bringing about the fall of our first parents, it follows, therefore, that he must also participate in the curse. The enmity between the serpent and mankind will continue until the final overthrow of Satan's power when the Messiah shall come, who is spoken of as the pacifactor (Shiloh, Genesis 49:10) and the Prince of Peace (Sar Shalom, Isaiah 9:6), who will, by crushing Satan's head, restore again the original peace and happiness.[1]

In Romans 16:20, it is said: "And the God of peace shall bruise Satan under your feet shortly." "Seed" is in Scripture used for the offspring of posterity; "her seed" therefore, denotes her posterity, including of course, the Messiah, the greatest of all her descendants, who by way of eminence and in allusion to this promise, is called THE SEED (Gal. 3:19),

[1] The Palestinian Targum testifies that in Genesis 3:15 there is promised a healing of the bite in the heel from the serpent, which is to take place "at the end of the days, in the days of King Messiah." In Bereshith rabba XII, the Midrash to Genesis, we read: "The things which God created perfect since man sinned have become corrupt and do not return to their proper condition until the son of Perez (see Gen. 38:29, Ruth 4:18, the Messiah out of the tribe of Judah) comes." According to this the Messiah is Saviour and Restorer.

who came to destroy the works of the Devil (Heb. 2:14), and who will:

1. Restore to man the Creator's moral image.
2. Restore communion and fellowship with God.
3. Remove the curse from man's heritage.
4. Conquer death in behalf of all mankind.

II. The Blessing of Noah

The Noah prophetic declaration in Genesis 9:26, 27, reads: "Blessed be the God of Shem; and Canaan shall be a servant of him. God will enlarge Japheth, and he shall dwell in the tents of Shem; and Canaan shall be a servant to him."

A. Shem. The words "Blessed be the God of Shem," imply that God was "the God of Shem" in a special manner, and is connected with special privileges. And, accordingly, we find that through the family of Shem was preserved the true worship of God with ISRAEL AS THE CHOSEN NATION, the "peculiar treasure" of God (Ex. 19:5).

B. Ham. The curse pronounced against Ham, or Canaan, began to be fulfilled in the time of Joshua. It was in his time that they were first brought under the yoke of the Shemites, and the conquest was afterward completed by Solomon (II Chron. 8:7, 8).

C. Japheth. The prophetic declaration relating to Japheth, comprises two parts: The first part, "God shall enlarge Japheth." This prediction commenced to have its fulfillment during his lifetime. Japheth had *seven children,* while Shem had *five* and Ham only *four.* The descendants of Japheth spread over the whole of Europe and a considerable part of Asia, and as some would have it, they probably crossed over to America by the Bering Strait. The second part in this prophetic utterance is, "And he shall dwell in the tents of Shem." According to the Chaldee Version (Targum), this is to be consummated when the Messiah comes, then the descendants of Japheth will join Israel in the worship of the

Almighty, and both would look upon Jerusalem as the spiritual center of all nations. Is this not in line with God's plan for the world? Compare Psalm 22:28; Isaiah 2:2-4; Zephaniah 3:10; Zechariah 8:20-23; 14:16. At that time God will exclaim: "Blessed be *Egypt* my people, and *Assyria* the work of my hands, and Israel my inheritance" (Isa. 19:25). "On that day," you will note, the curse resting upon the descendants of Ham will be removed, and they, with the descendants of Japheth will bow down before the Lord.

The second Messianic prophecy, like the first (Gen. 3), is a blessing which springs up in contrast to a curse. Sin and shame are the occasion of this prophecy. The sin is against Noah who, according to the rabbis, "was righteous in his own generation."[2] The shame is in the evil conduct of his son Ham.

> The blessing and the curse give a fresh glance into the history of mankind — a history which is not only a struggle against evil spirits with the assurance of an eventual victory, but is also a struggle between three great races of mankind.

III. The Seed of Abraham

Reference to the promise made to Abraham is found in Genesis 12:1-3, in connection with the call of separation, and the heart and soul of this call is God's great desire to bless all the families of the earth:

> Now the Lord said unto Abram, Get thee out of thy country, and from thy kindred, and from thy father's house, unto the land that I will show thee: and I will make of thee a great nation, and I will bless thee, and make thy name great; and be thou a blessing; and I will bless them that will bless thee, and him that curseth thee will I curse; and in thee shall all the families of the earth be blessed (Gen. 12:1-3).

This is more than the promise of "The Hope of a Pros-

---

[2] Noah is the first mediator of the Sacred history, a mediator of comfort. *Nechama* (Comfort) is one of the pregnant words in which all that is hoped from the God of salvation is combined. *Menachem* (Comforter) is a rabbinical designation for the Messiah. See Isaiah 49:13; 52:9; 61:2; John 14:16; Franz Delitzsch, etc., etc.

perous Era." It is a promise of the coming of a "Personal Messiah," and it distinctly refers to Christ, if we take the word of such men as Paul and Peter, and this we gladly do, because these men, like the Old Testament prophets, were inspired by God and therefore are true prophets of the true God (see Acts 3:25, 26; Gal. 3:8, 9, 14, 16, 29).

In order to understand the full meaning of this promise to Abraham, we must examine two other predictions that were made at the same time:

A. The promise was made that the Lord will bless all nations through his seed. Here we may ask: Has the world been blessed, in the way and to the extent contemplated in this promise? No one will deny the fact that Israel as a nation has been a blessing to the nations. This is beautifully and most convincingly stated by Paul in his letter to the Romans (9, 10, 11). Israel is still being used of God as His witness among the nations of the world. But the promise, that *all nations* shall be blessed in his *seed,* is something that we must look for in the future, when Israel as a nation will recognize the Lord Jesus as Messiah and Lord over all. At that time to come "ten men shall . . . take hold of the skirt of him that is a Jew, saying, We will go with you: for we heard that God is with you" (Zech. 8:23).

B. In this promise there is also the assurance given to Abraham, "thy seed shall possess the gates of his enemies" (Gen. 22:17). Historically we know that at no time in the past has this promise been realized. "The football of the nations" has been kicked about for many centuries and at no time since 70 A.D. has this nation possessed the gate of their enemies. Therefore, I do not believe that *seed* in these passages primarily refers to Abraham's literal descendants. *The primary meaning of these passages unquestionably is that of an individual,* "The Seed" of Abraham, who shall bring this universal blessing to a world under the curse of sin.

IV. JUDAH THE ROYAL AND MESSIANIC TRIBE

The Messianic promise contained in the blessing of Judah has always arrested the attention of Bible students. The reading of it will justify this unceasing interest. Jacob, you will remember, is on his deathbed. The Spirit allows him to get a glimpse of the future, and as he blesses his sons he selects Judah as the one through whom the promised Messiah would come:

> Judah, thee shall thy brethren praise;
> Thy hand shall be on the neck of thine enemies;
> Thy father's sons shall bow down before thee.
> Judah is a lion's whelp;
> From the prey, my son, thou art gone up.
> He stooped down, he crouched as a lion,
> And as a lioness; who shall rouse him up?
> The sceptre shall not depart from Judah,
> Nor the ruler's staff from between his feet,
> Until Shiloh come;
> And unto him shall the obedience of the peoples be.
>
> (Gen. 49:8-10, J.P.S.)

The blessing of Judah like that of his elder brothers commences with his own experience, looks on to the future of the tribe, and finds its highest fulfillment in his noblest Son, the Lord Jesus Christ.

"Judah, thou art he whom thy brethren shall praise." Here again play is put on the name, Judah, "Jehovah is praised," as we see from Genesis 29:35. When Leah gave birth to this her fourth son, she exclaimed with gratitude, "This time will I praise Jehovah, therefore she called his name Judah."

A. Judah was by no means perfect, but he had some good traits of character. It was at his suggestion that Joseph was not put to death by his brethren. Hear how he pleads with them:

"What profit is it if we slay our brother and conceal his blood? Come and let us sell him to the Ishmaelites, and let not our hands be upon him, for he is our brother, our flesh; and his brethren harkened unto him" (Gen. 37:26,27).

He thus saved the life of Joseph.

B. He also seemed to have had greater influence with his father as witnessed in connection with his plea to permit them to take their brother Benjamin to Egypt:

"Send the lad with me, and we will arise and go; that we may live, and not die, both we, and thou, and also our little ones. I will be surety for him; of my hand shalt thou require him: if I bring him not unto thee, and set him before thee, then let me bear the blame forever" (Gen. 43:8,9). Jacob then consented.

C. Judah had many worthy descendants who foreshadowed the Lord Jesus. There was Bezaleel, a man fit for the work of the Tabernacle, and thus typified the Lord Jesus Who is building the spiritual Tabernacle composed of living stones. Then there is Caleb, the faithful man of God who with Joshua insisted, contrary to the other spies, that the Lord is true even if all men be liars (Josh. 14:7-12). We also think of Boaz, the gracious kinsman redeemer, who by his marriage united to himself Ruth, the Gentile, who had been alienated from the commonwealth of Israel and estranged from the covenant of promise. And of course we also think of David, and his son, Solomon (Shelomo), and the other good kings who were of the tribe of Judah. All these heroes, however, sink into insignificance before the greatest Son of that tribe, the Lord Jesus, the Shiloh of this prophecy.

While the entire passage of Genesis 49:8-10 leads on to Christ, verse ten especially points as with a finger to Him upon whom depend the blessing and prosperity, not only of the tribe of Judah, but also of all mankind:

"The scepter shall not depart from Judah, nor a law-giver from between his feet, until Shiloh come; and unto Him shall be the obedience of the people."

The rabbis of old, though not agreeing with each other

as to the meaning of the root Shiloh, were almost unanimous in applying the term to the Messiah.

Targum Onkelos, who was a pupil of Gamaliel and to this day highly regarded among the Jews, renders it thus: "One having dominion shall not depart from Judah, nor a scribe from his children's children forever, 'ad d'yethe m'shichah,' until the Messiah comes, whose is the kingdom, and him the nations shall obey."

Targum Jerusalem interprets it thus: "Kings shall not fail from the House of Judah, nor skilful teachers of the Law from his children's children, until the time that the King Messiah come, and whom the nations shall serve."

The Peshito or Syrian Version, one of the oldest translations of the Bible, has this passage translated: "The sceptre shall not fail from Judah, nor an expounder from his feet, until he come whose right it is and to whom the kingdom belongs, and for him the nations shall wait."

It is evident from those ancient translations and interpretations that this prophecy points to an individual, and not to a town by the name Shiloh, in Ephraim, or to a like name anywhere else. An honored Hebrew Christian, the late David Baron, summarizes the opinion of scholars past and present in the following words:

> With regards to this prophecy, the first thing I want to point out is that all antiquity agrees in interpreting it of a personal Messiah. That is the view of the LXX version; The Targums of Onkelos, Jonathan, and Jerusalem; the Talmud; the Sohar; "Bereshith Rabba"; and, among modern Jewish commentators, even of Rashi, who say, "Until Shiloh come, that is King Messiah, whose is the kingdom." (*Rays of Messianic Glory,* page 258.)

Israel's existence as a nation began with the coming of Moses. With his coming there also came a revived hope in the coming of a Messiah. This hope, kept alive from the days of Adam till the death of Jacob, had no place in the hearts and minds of the children of Israel during their Egyptian bondage. Egypt was no place for the continuation of this hope. But God, remembering the covenant He had made with their fathers, said: "I have seen the affliction of My people, I have heard their cry, I know their sorrows, I am come down to deliver them out of the hand of the Egyptians, and to bring them up unto a good land" (Ex. 3:7,8). For this great work Moses was chosen, a personality who towers above all other great men of the Bible. Hence when God desired to revive the hope of the coming of the promised Messiah He used His beloved servant Moses as a type of the Coming One.

V. The Prophet Like Moses

This prophecy reads:

> The Lord thy God will raise up unto thee a Prophet from the midst of thee, of thy brethren, like unto me; unto him ye shall hearken; according to all that thou desiredst of the Lord thy God in Horeb in the day of the assembly, saying, Let me not hear again the voice of the Lord my God, neither let me see this great fire any more, that I die not. And the Lord said unto me, They have well said that which they have spoken. I will raise them up a Prophet from among their brethren, like unto thee; and I will put my words in his mouth, and he shall speak unto them all that I shall command him. And it shall come to pass, that whosoever will not hearken unto my words which he shall speak in my name, I will require of him (Deut. 18:15-19).

Says the great Franz Delitzsch,

> The prophecy indicates a definite prophet. It indicates a single person; and the history of the following period confirms the view, that the characteristic marks of the one in contradistinction to the many, which the concluding section (Deut. 18:20ff) presupposes, are involved in words "like me" and "like thee." For all the prophets who followed Moses are not mediators of such a revelation as the Sinaitic; but the divine revelation which is like the Sinaitic lies for all in the domain of the future, and their duty will consist in representing the spirit of the Sinaitic divine revelation, and thus preparing the way for a future divine revelation, whose mediator is to be the predicted prophet like Moses.

This passage, Deuteronomy 18:15-19, like the Messianic promises in Genesis, was generally interpreted by the religious leaders of the past as Messianic. Rabbi Levi ben Gershon states it thus: "In fact the Messiah is such a prophet as it is stated in the Midrash on the verse, 'Behold my servant shall prosper . . .' Moses by the miracles which he wrought drew but a single nation to the worship of God, *but the Messiah will draw all nations to the worship of God.*" Iben Ezra (1092-1167 A.D.) considers it possible that Joshua is intended and in Jalkut the view is held that Jeremiah may be the one promised. The great Abrabanel (1437 A. D.) says, "There was a common saying among the ancient Hebrews that the 'Messiah shall be exalted above Abraham, lifted up above Moses, and be higher than the angels of the ministry.'"

Going back to the days of Jesus we note that when the widow's son was raised from the dead, fear fell upon those that witnessed the miracle, "and they glorified God, saying, A Great Prophet had arisen up among us; and, that God hath visited his people" (Luke 7:16). Again, when Jesus fed the five thousand, those who saw this performed exclaimed, "This is of a truth that prophet that should come into the world" (John 6:14). When Jesus told the woman of Samaria about her shady past, the woman in wonderment said, "Sir, I perceive that thou art a prophet" (John 4:19). The use of the term "prophet" by the Jews of Jesus' day shows not only that they expected the Messiah to be a prophet in accordance with the promise in Deuteronomy eighteen, but also that He who performed these miracles was indeed that Promised Prophet. Well may Prof. Kurtz observe:

> Now a prophet like unto Moses, must necessarily, like him, be a redeemer of the people, a founder and executor of a New Covenant with God, and since a New Covenant is, by implication, a better covenant than that which preceded it, it follows that the prophet, "like unto Moses" is really greater than he was. Hence this prophecy applied in its fulness to no prophet

of the Old Testament. It is in Christ alone, the executor of the New Covenant, the Redeemer of all men, that this promise is perfectly and finally fulfilled (*Man of Sacred History*, p. 145).

In many points Moses was a type of Christ:

A. In his deliverance from a violent death in infancy.

B. In his years of silent training in the wilderness.

C. In his willingness to leave the palace of the king to become the redeemer of his people (Ex. 3:10).

D. In his work as a mediator between God and Israel (Ex. 19:16, 18; 20:18-20).

E. In his intercession in behalf of a sinful people (Ex. 32:7-14, 33; Num. 14:11-20). How exactly all these were fulfilled in Christ. Our rabbis in interpreting this passage personally and Messianically have indeed followed in the footsteps of all true prophets of God.

VI. The Star and Sceptre of Jacob

When we turn to the Book of Numbers we find a prophetic utterance by a heathen. In one of the Egyptian papyri there is a note of a certain dispatch which was sent out during the reign of Menephath to the King of Tyre. This message was entrusted to the care of Baal, the son of Zippor. This old papyrus, now in the British Museum, is a witness of the truth of the record before us. The name of the King of Moab and the city "by the river" have been identified by scholars.

Balaam had been called by Balak, King of Moab, to do something against the people of God who at that time had nearly reached the borders of Moab. This heathen prophet, perfectly willing for a good sum of money to curse Israel, cries out: "How shall I curse, whom God hath not cursed?" (Num. 23:8). This naturally was most displeasing to Balak. He took him to another position and insisted for another trial. Balaam made his second attempt against God's people and is moved to say that God does not change His mind and that he himself could not speak anything but that which God has commanded. Here are his words:

> He hath not beheld iniquity in Jacob;
> Neither hath he seen perverseness in Israel;
> The Lord his God is with him,
> And the shout of a king is among them.
> God bringeth them forth out of Egypt;
> He hath as it were the strength of the wild ox.
> Surely there is no enchantment with Jacob;
> Neither is any divination with Israel:
> Now shall it be said of Jacob and of Israel,
> What hath God wrought!
> Behold, the people riseth up as a lioness,
> And as a lion doth he lift himself up:
> He shall not lie down until he eat of the prey,
> And drink the blood of the slain.
>
> (Num. 23:21-24, R.V.)

This made Balak angry, but we note that he gives Balaam another chance to curse Israel. This third attempt however turns to be a real blessing:

> How goodly are thy tents, O Jacob, thy tabernacles, O Israel!
> As valleys are they spread forth,
> As gardens by the riverside,
> As lign-aloes which the Lord hath planted,
> As cedar-trees beside the waters.
> Water shall flow from his buckets,
> And his seed shall be in many waters,
> And his king shall be higher than Agag,
> And his kingdom shall be exalted.
> God bringeth him forth out of Egypt,
> He hath as it were the strength of the wild-ox:
> He shall eat up the nations his adversaries,
> And shall break their bones in pieces,
> And smite them through with his arrows.
> He couched, he lay down as a lion,
> And as a lioness; who shall rouse him up?
> Blessed be every one that blesseth thee,
> And cursed be every one that curseth thee.
>
> (Num. 24:5-9, R.V.)

Enraged, Balak ordered his hireling to return home. His services were of no good to him. He simply irritated him. But Balaam by this time had something to tell him and it was this, should the king give him a house full of silver and gold, he could not speak otherwise than as God commanded him. Then he begins to tell the king what would occur to his people in the latter days:

> I see him, but not now;
> I behold him, but not nigh;
> There shall come forth a star out of Jacob,
> And a sceptre shall rise out of Israel,
> And shall smite through the corners of Moab,
> And break down all the sons of tumult.
> And Edom shall be a possession,
> Seir also shall be a possession, who were his enemies;
> While Israel doeth valiantly.
> And out of Jacob shall one have dominion,
> And shall destroy the remnant from the city.
> (Num. 24:17-19, R.V.)

"A star goeth forth out of Jacob." This, and with what follows, is a more specific designation of the vision spoken of in the preceding part of the verse. A star is so natural an image of the greatness and splendor of rulers, that it is used by almost all nations. The birth and accession of the throne of great kings was believed to be often signalized by the unusual appearance of stars. The words *"a sceptre ariseth from Israel"* seems to be based upon Genesis 49:10: "The sceptre shall not depart from Judah, nor a lawgiver from between his feet until Shiloh come." In both places the sceptre is plainly an emblem of dominion. But, what was meant by this star and sceptre? Was this a designation to some particular king of Israel who was to appear, and make his reign glorious by the conquest of his enemies? So it has often been explained. But there is enough historical evidence to justify the statement that "no king of Israel is here specifically alluded to; the idea is, that dominion and a conquering power shall arise in Israel, and that this dominion will reach its consummation only in the Messiah."

Of whom does Balaam speak so joyfully, "I shall see him,

but not now?" Of course of the one spoken of under the figure of the "Star" that is to come out of Jacob. Were we to ask our forefathers and the religious leaders of their day they would tell us that they regarded Balaam's prophecy as a forecast of King Messiah. This was the interpretation of the Targums Onkelos and Jonathan, also Mammonides and Rashi. Rashi regards it as a double prophecy, as having its partial fulfillment in David, and its complete fulfillment in the Messiah. The extent of this belief is evident from the fact that in the year 132 A.D., when a false Messiah appeared, Rabbi Akibba called him Bar-Kocheda, son of the star, an evident echo of Numbers 24:17. But when his attempted revolt against Rome failed and five hundred thousand Jews were slaughtered, his name was changed to Bar-Kozebiah, son of a lie.

The fundamental idea of this prophecy seems to be the victory over the heathen world, as represented by the nations mentioned in the subsequent verses. But this could not be said to have been achieved by any one of the kings of Israel. After David's victories over the Moabites, for example, they soon recovered, and again annoyed Israel and were again the subjects of severe threatening. Neither could all of the kings of Israel be said to have achieved a victory over the heathen, which seems to be commensurate with the spirit and design of this prophecy. Indeed the kingdom of Israel, for all the purposes which it was designed to accomplish, was, without the Messiah, but a trunk without a head. The reign of the anointed One, the Priest-king, was the great glory which was foretold to patriarch and prophet, at first but indistinctly, but more and more clearly, as the fulness of time for his appearing approached.

Our Lord Jesus clearly refers to this prophecy when He says of Himself: "I am the root and offspring of David, the bright and morning star" (Rev. 22:16).

The star has always been the guiding influence of those

who held on to the hope of the coming of the Messiah. The wise men from the east followed the star, and when they reached Bethlehem and the Babe, they asked: "Where is he that is born King of the Jews? for we have seen his star in the east, and are come to worship him" (Matt. 2:2). Peter reminds us that "We have also a more sure word of prophecy; whereunto ye do well that ye take heed, as unto a light that shineth in a dark place, until the day dawn, and the day star arise in your hearts" (II Pet. 1:19).

Chapter II

MESSIANIC PROPHECY IN THE HISTORICAL BOOKS
(Joshua through Kings)

The historical books of Joshua and Judges do not add much to the picture of the Messiah. There are, however, a few important links to the chain of events which run on till the appearance of the Messiah. Joshua records the appearance of the Captain of the Lord's Host, the promise of victory, and the conquest of the land. The book closes with an exhortation to the people who are reminded that it is God who fought for them, and that they should serve Him with all their heart (23:6-11). The Book of Judges on the other hand tells of the failure of God's people. It is one of the darkest periods in Israel's history. In Judges 2:11-14, 16, we are given a summary of the whole book:

> And the children of Israel did evil in the sight of the Lord, and served Baalim; and they forsook the Lord God of their fathers, who brought them out of the land of Egypt, and followed other gods, of the gods of the peoples that were around about them, and bowed themselves down unto them, and provoked the Lord to anger. And they forsook the Lord, and served Baal and Ashtaroth. And the anger of the Lord was kindled against them, and He delivered them into the hands of spoilers that spoiled them, and He sold them into the hands of their enemies round about. . . . Nevertheless the Lord raised up judges, who delivered them out of the hands of those that spoiled them.

What a picture of God's grace and continued patience! Jehovah did not forsake them. Nor did all Israel turn away from Him. In the midst of lawlessness and idolatry there were still those who feared God and waited for the fulfillment of His promises. In the Book of Ruth we meet a lovely Moabitess, one hundred years before David, and we see God at work preparing for the coming of the king out of whose loins, in the fullness of time, there is to arise one who is to be the Messiah of Israel and the Saviour of the world.

The words of Hannah in the form of a song, as recorded in I Samuel 2:1-10, echo the same sentiments and longing of the people of that time:

> My heart rejoiceth in the Lord,
> Mine horn is exalted in the Lord:
> My mouth is enlarged over mine enemies;
> Because I rejoice in thy salvation. . . .
> The adversaries of the Lord shall be broken in pieces,
> Out of heaven shall He thunder upon them:
> The Lord shall judge the ends of the earth;
> And he shall give strength unto his king,
> And will exalt the horn of his Anointed. (vv. 1, 10.)

Prof. Franz Delitzsch says,

> We do not deny the possibility that the song may have been assigned to her by a historian, but we deny decidedly that it does not harmonize with her position and feelings, and that therefore it could not be composed by her. And why should not Hannah, who had borne Samuel under her heart, the founder of the school of the prophets, who anointed David the sweet singer of Israel, not have the gift of poetry? Or must we think of David in the mention which is made of the *divinely anointed one,* so that the close of the song expresses a hope out of David's age assigned to the time of the judges, and which therefore excludes Hannah's authorship?

Prof. Delitzsch is right. So are all the interpreters of Scripture who prefer to let God be God in the revelation of His plan of salvation. Whatever else Hannah had in mind during her period of prayer and meditation of this we are quite certain, that in the mind of Hannah there stands before her an ideal king whom Jehovah has appointed, and through whom He will bring final victory over all His enemies and establish the Messianic kingdom, or, "the raising up of the kingdom of God in His Christ" (Messiah).

THE MESSIAH A DESCENDANT OF DAVID

David is the outstanding figure of that age and the one who was chosen to become the vehicle of Messianic expression, a notable torchbearer in the long procession of this hope. With him God made a covenant, which four generations later, Jeremiah declared could never be broken (Jer. 33:17, 18, 20-22). The record of this covenant is found in II Samuel 7:11-16:

> Moreover, the Lord telleth thee that the Lord will make thee an house when thy days be fulfilled, and thou shalt sleep with thy fathers, I will set up thy seed after thee which shall proceed out of thy bowels, and I will establish his kingdom. He shall build an house for my name, and I will establish the throne of his kingdom for ever. I will be his father, and he shall be my son: if he commit iniquity I will chasten him with the rod of men and with the stripes of the children of men; but my mercy shall not depart from him, as I took it from Saul, whom I put away before thee, and thine house and thy kingdom shall be made sure for ever before thee: thy throne shall be established for ever.

This was the foundation stone upon which the Jews built up their expectation, that, come what might to the nation, to its city and its polity, there would always be a king, ready to appear in God's good time, a king who should belong to the stock and lineage of David.

We find many of the prophets picked up the same thought and continued to build on the same foundation-text. Jeremiah writes: "They shall serve the Lord their God, and David their king, whom I will raise up unto them" (Jer. 30:9). So also Ezekiel: "And I will set up one shepherd over them, and he shall feed them, even my servant David; he shall feed them, and he shall be their shepherd. And I the Lord will be their God, and my servant David a prince among them; I the Lord have spoken it" (Ezek. 34:23, 24). Similarly, he adds later: "And my servant David shall be king over them; . . . and David my servant shall be their prince for ever" (Ezek. 37:24, 25).

Listen to Isaiah: "I will make an everlasting covenant with you, even the sure mercies of David. Behold, I have given him for a witness to the peoples, a leader and commander to the peoples"[1] (Isa. 55:3, 4). In the eighty-ninth Psalm, a Maschil of Ethan, he reminds coreligionists of God's Covenant promises:

> I have found David my servant; with my holy oil have I anointed him: with whom my hand shall be established: mine arm also shall strengthen him. The enemy shall not exact upon him; nor the son of wickedness afflict him. And I will beat down his foes before his face, and plague them that hate him. But my faithfulness and my mercy shall be with him; and in my name shall his horn be exalted. I will set his hand also in the sea, and his right hand in the rivers. He shall cry unto me, Thou art my Father, my God, and the rock of my salvation. Also I will make him my first-born, higher than the kings of the earth. My mercy will I keep for him for evermore, and my covenant shall stand fast with him. His seed also will I make to endure for ever, and his throne as the days of heaven. . . . My covenant will I not break, nor alter the thing that is gone out of my lips. Once have I sworn by my holiness, that I will not lie unto David; his seed shall endure for ever, and his throne as the sun before me. It shall be established for ever as the moon, and as a faithful witness in heaven (Ps. 89:20-29, 34-37).

Such words as these forbid in themselves fulfillment in David, or in any mere son of David.[2] They lead one immediately and directly to the King of kings on an eternal throne. Unless they have been realized in Jesus, the Covenant with David has been broken, and we must change the words in this and in all other promises God has made concerning the coming of the Messiah.

[1] "The peoples" are non-Jewish.

[2] We can understand how David should have been profoundly impressed, if he had taken these words in a strictly literal sense. That this is too narrow an interpretation is evident from his own life and writings.

The Davidic Covenant does not annul, or forget the covenants made with Adam and Eve and Abraham. It holds its close contact with them in the use of the word "Seed." The apostle Paul, in his letter to the Galatians (3:17), introduces a lengthy argument as he tries to show that the covenant with Abraham was not annuled by the introduction of the Mosaic Law, but is, on the contrary, the covenant under which all believers are now the seed of Abraham and heirs to the promise: "In thy seed shall all the nations of the earth be blessed," which promise is fulfilled in Christ.

The Seed of the woman which shall defeat the serpent and the Seed of Abraham in whom all the nations will be blessed, now becomes the son of David, a Royal Person whose throne is everlasting. In this light only are we to understand and interpret such Messianic prophecies as Psalms 2, 45, 72, 110; Isaiah 11; Jeremiah 37:31,32; Ezekiel 34, 36 and 37. The fundamental idea of all these prophecies is the perpetuity of David's kingdom, and its final ascendancy over all the earth.

A final glance of David into the future is recorded in II Samuel 23:1-7. He has come to the end of his life on earth and as he looks back he is prompted to give thanks to God for having delivered him from both internal and external foes. The Spirit of God inspired him to commit in writing his gratitude and thanksgiving (see II Sam. 23 and Ps. 18). At the conclusion of his song of praise he is led to make his final declaration concerning the coming of the Messiah:

> Now these are the last words of David:
> David the son of Jesse saith,
> And the man who was raised up on high,
> And the anointed of the God of Jacob,
> And the sweet psalmist of Israel said,
>
> The Spirit of the Lord spake by me,
> And his word was upon my tongue.
> The God of Israel said,
> The Rock of Israel spake to me;

One that ruleth over men righteously,
That ruleth in the fear of God,
He shall be as the light of the morning, when the sun riseth,
A morning without clouds;
As the tender grass springing out of the earth,
Through clear shining after rain.

Although my house is not so with God;
Yet hath He made with me an everlasting covenant
Ordered in all things and sure;
For this is all my salvation, and all my desire,
Although he make it not to grow.

But the ungodly (Belial) shall be all of them as thorns
    to be thrust away,
Because they cannot be taken with the hand;
But the man that toucheth them
Must be armed with iron and the staff of a spear;
And they shall be utterly burned with fire in their place.

The following from Keil's Commentary on the Books of Samuel will help us to understand this great oracle of chapter 23:1-7.

A. *The introduction.* Verses one and two call to our attention the fact that David must have been acquainted with the prophecies of Balaam as recorded in Numbers 24:15-24.

B. *The king and his kingdom.* In verses three, four and five we find a vision of the king and his kingdom and at the same time an acknowledgment of his own failure. (See Jer. 23:5, 6; Zech. 9:9, 10).

C. *The wicked have no hope,* verses six and seven.

This is the vision he saw for the future: He saw one of his descendants ruling the world in righteousness. His government is compared to a cloudless, perfect day. By faith David saw his hopes for eternity centered in the Great Coming One. At His appearance the wicked will be destroyed. Then peace, the peace for which a sin-sick, war-stricken world is yearning, shall be established. God's peace will be ushered in by the Prince of Peace. To Him every knee is to bow. He is to reign forever and ever. This is the successor to David's throne.

CHAPTER III

MESSIANIC PROPHECY IN THE PSALMS

"Rejoice in the Lord, O ye righteous: for praise is comely for the upright." In this quotation from Psalm 33:1 we have a concise and satisfactory definition of the Psalms. The Book of Psalms was the Hymn Book (Theilim) of ancient Israel. In these songs the people poured out their prayers and petitions and gave voice to their sorrows and joys. Much of their history, their successes and defeats, can be traced in this book. When the nation was plunged into sorrow because of their capture at the hands of the Babylonians they expressed their sorrow in Psalm 137:

> By the rivers of Babylon, there we sat, yea, we wept,
> When we remembered Zion,
> We hanged our harps
> Upon the willows in the midst thereof.
> For there they that carried us away captive required of us mirth,
> Saying, Sing us one of the songs of Zion.
> How shall we sing the Lord's song
> In a strange land?
> If I forget thee, O Jerusalem,
> Let my right hand forget her cunning.
> If I do not remember thee,
> Let my tongue cleave to the roof of my mouth;
> If I prefer not Jerusalem above my chief joy. (Ps. 137:1-6.)

When that sorrow was changed into joy some seventy years later, they professed that joy in the glad song of Psalm one-hundred twenty-six:

> When the Lord turned again the captivity of Zion,
> We were like them that dream.
> Then was our mouth filled with laughter,

And our tongue with singing:
Then said they among the heathen,
The Lord hath done great things for them.
The Lord hath done great things for us;
Whereof we are glad.   (Ps. 126:1-3.)

The Psalter is the jewel-case from which the saints of God obtain rare and precious gems of thought and spiritual strength to comfort and stimulate them on their journey along life's pathway. If in trouble they pray in the words of the forty-second Psalm. When they are glad, they give thanks to God for His goodness; in times of their distress, in the words of Psalm forty-six:

Let the waters rage and foam!
Let the mountains quake at the proud swelling thereof!
Jehovah of hosts is with us,
The God of Jacob is our high fortress.

A purely secular psalm is not found anywhere in the book. It was and continues to be the devotional manual adapted to express and guide the religious life of God's people. It can safely be said that no other nation has produced such a body of literature of such character. Other nations have produced poems of great beauty, having for their themes the wonders and beauty of nature, the acts, ambitions, aspirations, passions and sorrows of man, but few concerning God and His great plan of salvation.

In the Book of Psalms there are poems that speak of the revelation of God in nature: Psalms 8; 19:1-6; 29; 104; 148; of God's revelation in history: Psalms 78; 105; 114; and of God's revelation in and through His Torah (Law): Psalms 19:7-14; 119. There are also psalms that speak of the attributes of God — that He is One, Near, Good, Holy and Just: Psalms 23; 29; 33; 34; 36; 90; 103 and 104.

But there is more in the book than these. Throughout it there runs the divine revelation of the purpose and program of God for Israel and through Israel for the whole world. Believing as we do in the authority and unity of the Scriptures, we naturally expect to find intimations, inferences and direct statements concerning the Messianic hope in the Psalms. In this we are not disappointed. Like all the other books of the Old Testament, the Psalms find their highest and most complete realization in the Lord Jesus Christ.

When the Lord Jesus revealed Himself to the disciples after the Resurrection, "He said unto them, These are the words which I spoke unto you, while I was yet with you, that all things must be fulfilled, which were written in the law of Moses (Torah), and in the prophets (Neviim), and in the psalms (Theilim — a part of the Ketubim), concerning me" (Luke 24:44). Here the Lord is saying to His disciples that the whole of the Old Testament has many things concerning His person, His life, ministry, death and resurrection and His coming again. Many of the chief features of His career are predicted in the Psalms.

I. THE MESSIAH'S ADVENT AND ITS PURPOSE
(Psalms 40; 69; 70)

In these psalms we have a description of a sufferer who is fully consecrated to God and His service. His suffering is at the hands of people who by birth and training should belong to God and in His service:

> Sacrifice and offering thou didst not desire;
> Mine ears hast thou opened;
> Burnt offering and sin offering hast thou not required.
> Then said I, Lo, I come;
> In the volume of the book it is written of me,
> I delight to do thy will, O my God.   (Ps. 40:6-8.)

> Because for thy sake I have borne reproach;
> Shame hath covered my face.
> I am become a stranger unto my brethren,
> And an alien unto my mother's children.
> For the zeal of thy house hath eaten me up;
> And the reproaches of them that reproach thee are
>   fallen upon me.   (Ps. 69:7-9.)

He looked for pity, but there was none. He was mocked by words and cruel deeds. He suffered intense thirst and they gave him vinegar and gall for his nourishment. He is sore sick but his steadfast faith in God for deliverance is sure. As to his enemies, they will be put to shame and be confounded, while he proclaims deliverance to the joy of all who seek God and look for his salvation (Pss. 69; 70).

II. THE MESSIAH'S SONSHIP AND BIRTH
(Psalm 2)

That this psalm is Messianic is proven by Jewish and Christian tradition. In Matthew 26:63, the high priest asks Jesus whether he were the Messiah, the Son of God, and by so doing borrows two appellations from the Old Testament expectations of the coming Messiah. In John 1:49, Nathaniel uses a reference found in this psalm as he greets Jesus, saying, "Thou art the Son of God: thou art the King of Israel." Again, in the prayer of Peter and John as recorded in Acts 4:23-28, reference is made to this psalm. David, then, wrote this psalm, and he wrote it no doubt at the time some local happening affected him. But whatever the local coloring we know the psalm reaches into our own day and far into the future.

> Why do the heathen rage,
> And the people imagine a vain thing?

The psalmist is amazed at it. God is laughing at the folly of the nations, and the Son is speaking of their defeat. "Psalm 2," says Dr. Briggs, "represents the Messiah enthroned on Zion at the right hand of God as His Son, citing the divine decree entitling him to the position, with all the prerogatives of universal and everlasting sovereignty." Here are the words that can have no other interpretation:

> Jehovah said unto me, Thou art my Son;
> This day I have begotten thee.
> Ask of me,

And I shall give the nations for thine inheritance,
And the uttermost parts of the earth for thy possession.
(Ps. 2:7, 8.)

The Messiah is to possess the uttermost parts of the earth and subdue his enemies. His first coming has already done so in a measure, but this is just a foreshadowing of things yet to come. This may come sooner than some of us think.

III. The Messiah's Deity and Humanity
(Psalms 45; 110)

The psalmist here speaks of a king in godlike majesty. Who is this distinguished personality? The poet describing the glories of the bridegroom and the splendors of the bridal ceremony is moved by the Spirit to recognize him as the one who came to claim a throne and reign forever and ever:

My heart is inditing [bubbling over] a good matter:
I speak of things which I have made touching the king;
My tongue is the pen of a ready writer.
Thou art fairer than the children of men;
Grace is poured into thy lips;
Therefore God hath blessed thee for ever.
Gird thy sword upon thy thigh, O most mighty,
With thy glory and thy majesty,
And in thy majesty ride prosperously
Because of truth and meekness and righteousness;
And thy right hand shall teach thee fearful things.
Thine arrows are sharp
In the heart of the king's enemies;
Peoples fall under thee.
Thy throne, O God, is for ever and ever;
A sceptre of equity is the sceptre of thy kingdom.
Thou hast loved righteousness, and hated wickedness;
Therefore God, thy God, hath anointed thee
With the oil of gladness above thy fellows. (Ps. 45:1-7.)

"Whether this psalm has, or had, a local application," says Dr. G. Campbell Morgan, "or is wholly idealistic, cannot be certainly determined. It matters very little, for it is one of the songs which inevitably is Messianic in its deepest and fullest meaning."

The writer of Hebrews quotes this psalm to prove the exaltation of Christ above the angels, saying:

"And again, when he bringeth in the first-born into the world, he saith, And let the angels of God worship him. And of the angels he saith, who maketh his angels spirits, and his ministers a flame of fire. But of the Son he saith, Thy throne, O God, is forever and ever: a sceptre of righteousness is the sceptre of thy kingdom" (Heb. 1:6-8).

The Messianic interpretation therefore is sufficiently justified and in line with such Commentators as Iben Ezra, David Kimchi and others. The Messiah, as the Son of God, bears divine majesty and reflects the divine glory. David's son and David's Lord — Son of Man and Son of God.

> The Lord saith unto my lord, Sit thou at my right hand,
> Until I make thine enemies thy footstool.
> The Lord shall send forth the rod of thy strength out of Zion;
> Rule thou in the midst of thine enemies.
> Thy people offer themselves willingly in the day of thy power;
> In the beauties of holiness, from the womb of the morning,
> Thou hast the dew of thy youth.
> The Lord hath sworn, and will not repent,
> Thou art a priest for ever
> After the order of Melchizedek.
> The Lord at thy right hand
> Shall strike through kings in the day of his wrath.
> He shall judge among the nations,
> He shall fill [the places] with dead bodies;
> He shall strike through the head in many countries.
> He shall drink of the brook in the way;
> Therefore shall he lift up the head.   (Ps. 110.)

We can never exhaust the treasuries of the Book of Psalms. A well-known Bible teacher, E. C. Olson, gave 204 radio messages on the Psalms, and each message took twenty minutes radio time, but he spent not less than four hours preparing each message. The famous Dr. Spurgeon of London wrote seven large volumes, two and a third million words, on this book! How much spiritual wealth there is in the Book of Psalms!

The Psalms enjoy a world-wide reputation because they contain not only a profound revelation of the inner life of Israel but express the longing and yearning of the human heart. Israel's Messianic hope as expressed in numerous Psalms describes One "manifested in the flesh" Who is to come to redeem man and to establish His reign on earth. We wish at this time to meditate on:

IV. THE MESSIAH'S BETRAYAL AND CRUCIFIXION
(Psalms 41: 9, 11; 22; 34:20)

"Unless the apostles," says Dr. J. A. Huffman, "with Peter as their spokesman, were mistaken in their interpretation of the forty-first Psalm when a successor to Judas was chosen (Acts 1:16), the betrayal of Jesus is portrayed here."[1]

> Yea, mine own familiar friend, in whom I trusted, which did
>   eat my bread,
> Hath lifted up his heel against me.
> But this I know that thou delightest in me,
> Because mine enemy doth not triumph over me.
>   (Ps. 41:9, 11.)

"I speak not of you all," said Jesus to His disciples who partook with Him the Last Supper, "I know whom I have chosen: but that the Scripture may be fulfilled, he that eateth bread with me hath lifted up his heel against me" (John 13:18).

The twenty-second Psalm begins with a shriek of anguish and goes on with a cry for help, full of trust, and ends with thanksgiving and the vision of the world-wide kingdom of God from the suffering of the One whose language is heard:

> My God, my God, why hast thou forsaken me?
> Why art thou so far from helping me, and from the words
>   of my groaning?   (Ps. 22:1.)

---

[1] The Messianic Hope in both Testaments.

All they that see me laugh me to scorn:
They shoot out the lip, they shake the head saying,
Commit thyself to Jehovah; let him deliver him:
Let him rescue him, seeing he delighted in him.

(Ps. 22:7, 8.)

The psalmist refers to the tribulations that continued for a time; but certainly in neither the biography of David, nor any other suffering one known to us, is there an experience to equal that of the sorrow and anguish described here. David's enemies never parted his garments (v. 18), and could never expect any deliverance of his to be the cause of the conversion of all nations to Jehovah as described in verse twenty-seven; while to none other than the Messiah could the confident anticipations of universal conquest, as the result of his present suffering be applied.

In the New Testament this psalm is regarded as Messianic. It is sacred to Christians because it is so closely related to the Crucified One. Here is Matthew's version of it:

And they that passed by reviled him, wagging their heads and saying, Thou that destroyest the temple, and buildest it in three days, save thyself. If thou be the Son of God, come down from the cross. In like manner also the chief priests mocking him, with the scribes and elders, saying, He saved others; himself he cannot save. Let him now come down from the cross, and we will believe on him. He trusted in God; let him deliver him now, if he desireth him: for He said, I am the Son of God (Matt. 27:39-43).

John, describing the events of the Crucifixion (John 19:23, 24) in detail, informs us that:

The soldiers, when they had crucified Jesus, took his garments, and made four parts; to every soldier a part; and also the coat: But the coat was without seam, woven from the top throughout. They said therefore one to another, Let us not rend it, but cast lots for it, whose it shall be.

Then he adds these significant words: "That the Scripture might be fulfilled, which saith, 'They part my garments among them, and cast lots upon my vesture.'"

Augustine was quite right when he said, "This psalm was written concerning me." "Him who knew no sin He made to be sin for us, that we might be made the righteousness of God in Him" (II Cor. 5:21).

V. THE MESSIAH'S RESURRECTION
(Psalm 16)

G. Campbell Morgan, D. D., calls this:

> A song of satisfaction. The singer is not one who is unfamiliar with peril. The opening sentence is a sigh of revealing the consciousness thereof, and towards the close, the shadows of Sheol and the terror of corruption are recognized. Yet these things only find a place here that they may be cancelled by the facts which create a sense of triumph over all peril.[2]

Concerning the interpretation of Psalm 16 divers opinions have been held — from Davidson to Wolfe, who regards its Messianic import as easy and natural to perceive. The particular passages which touch the Resurrection are as follows:

> I have set Jehovah always before me:
> Because he is at my right hand, I shall not be moved.
> Therefore my heart is glad, and my glory rejoiceth:
> My flesh also shall dwell in safety,
> For thou wilt not leave my soul to Sheol;
> Neither wilt thou suffer thy holy one to see corruption (vv. 8-10).

The psalm is quoted by Peter in his Pentecostal sermon (Acts 2:22-28) where reference is made to His death and resurrection. Paul speaking at Antioch, said:

> And as concerning that he raised him from the dead, now no more to return to corruption, he said on this wise, I will give you the sure mercies of David. Wherefore he saith also in another psalm [sixteenth], Thou shalt not suffer thine Holy One to see corruption (Acts 13:34, 35),

and through whom men may be justified from all things from which they could not be justified by the law of Moses.

---

[2] G. Campbell Morgan, *Notes on the Psalms*, Revell Company, Publishers.

VI. The Messiah's Present Office as King-Priest
(Psalm 110)

There should be little question about the Messianic character of this psalm. In it there is a specific setting forth of the high priestly, as well as kingly, prerogatives of the Messiah.

> The Lord said unto my Lord,
> Sit thou on my right hand,
> Till I make thine enemies the footstool of thy feet.
> The Lord shall send the rod of thy strength out of Zion:
> Rule thou in the midst of thine enemies
> The Lord hath sworn and will not repent,
> Thou art a priest forever
> After the order of Melchizedek.   (Ps. 110:1, 2, 4.)

To whom does the psalm refer? To some historical king, or to the future Messiah?

Dr. Kirkpatrick states,

> If it could be considered by itself, apart from the New Testament use of it, we should have little hesitation in regarding it as addressed by some prophet to the reigning king, like Psalms 20, 21, 45. . . . Many who in every other case regard Messianic Psalms as having a primary historical meaning, feel that here our Lord's authority compels them to hold that this Psalm was written by David, and was addressed by him to the future Messiah, who, he believed, would spring from his family.[3]

Our Lord Jesus used it to prove His Messiahship on several occasions.

> While the Pharisees were gathered together, Jesus asked them a question, saying, What think ye of Christ? whose son is he? They say unto him, The son of David. He saith unto them, How then doth David in the Spirit call him Lord, saying,
>
>> The Lord said unto my Lord,
>> Sit thou on my right hand,
>> Till I put thine enemies underneath thy feet?
>
> If David then called him Lord, how is he his son? And no one was able to answer him a word, neither durst any man from that day forth ask him any more questions. (Matt. 22:41-46; see also Mark 12:36; Luke 20:42, 43.)

[3] A. F. Kirkpatrick, *The Book of Psalms*, p. 663.

The entire Epistle to the Hebrews is a commentary to this psalm. The rabbis fearing that this psalm interpreted as Messianic might be a lift to Christians, have tried their utmost to find some other subject that would satisfy its statement and have failed.[4] Franz Delitzsch recognizes this psalm as Messianic in the sense that it contains prophecy that points immediately to the person of a coming One who is to set up the kingdom of God on earth.

VII. THE MESSIAH'S COMING AGAIN — TO JUDGE AND TO REIGN (Psalms 2; 46; 72)

In Psalm two the world is in rebellion against God and His Son, Jesus Christ; humanity is like a heaving ocean, like a troubled sea which cannot rest. "The kings of the earth set themselves, and the rulers take counsel together, against the Lord, and against his anointed, saying, Let us break their bands asunder, and cast away their cords from us" (2:2,3). This is the spirit of lawlessness which in every age has resisted the authority of God and is culminating today, as never before, and which is to reach its full development in the coming of the lawless one. The world is hastening to its Armageddon, "to the battle of that great day of God Almighty."

The forty-sixth Psalm may have for its background the deliverance of Jerusalem from Sennacherib (701 B. C.), as some scholars think, or the victory given to Jehoshaphat over the Ammonites as suggested by Delitzsch and others. "Neither of these events exhausts the language here used by the psalmist," declares the Rev. E. Bender Samuel. Prophetically the psalmist is expressing a refrain in verses 7 and 11 —

"The Lord of hosts is with us;
The God of Jacob is our refuge," which is an echo of

---

[4] The Rev. G. Phillips, in his *Commentary on Psalms,* says, "By far the greater part of the elder rabbis have determined that it (Psalm 110) speaks of the Messiah." See Midrash Tehillim on Psalm 2, Venice edition. Also *Witness of the Psalms to Christ* by Bishop Alexander, p. 62.

Isaiah's great message about Immanuel (Isa. 7:14). It is also a look into the future to the last pre-millenial war, when the Lord Jesus will utterly destroy the enemies that will come up to fight against Israel and against God's Anointed One.

This terrible war is sure to come. Zechariah speaks of it most graphically:

> Behold, a day of the Lord cometh, when thy spoil shall be divided in the midst of thee. For I will gather all nations against Jerusalem to battle; and the city shall be taken, and the houses rifled, and the women ravished: and the half of the city shall go forth into captivity, and the residue of the people shall not be cut off from the city. Then shall the Lord go forth, and fight against those nations, as when He fought in the day of battle. And his feet shall stand in that day upon the Mount of Olives (Zech: 14:1-7).

The prophet Joel speaking on the same subject says in the name of God:

> Behold in those days and in that time, when I shall bring again the captivity of Judah and Jerusalem, I will gather all nations, and will bring them down into the valley of Jehoshaphat, and will plead with them there for my people and for my heritage Israel whom they have scattered among nations and parted my land. . . . Proclaim ye this among the nations; prepare war; stir up the mighty men; let all the men of war draw near, let them come up. Beat your plowshares into swords, and your pruning-hooks into spears, let the weak say I am strong. Haste ye and come all ye nations round about and gather yourselves together. . . . Jehovah shall roar from Zion, and utter His voice from Jerusalem and the heavens and the earth shall shake, but Jehovah will be a refuge unto His people, and a stronghold to the children of Israel (Joel 3:1, 2, 9-11, 16).

David Baron, a beloved Hebrew Christian Bible teacher of a former generation, has this to say concerning the events after the judgments:

> When the final judgments of God are abroad in the earth, and when the anti-Christian rage and persecution will be everywhere directed, not only against the confessors of Christ, but against those in Israel who are faithful to the God of their fathers,

there will be weeping, and mourning, and heart-searching among
the scattered tribes of Israel in all the lands of their dispersion.

And when at last, in the hour of their deepest need, their
long rejected, crucified Messiah appears for their deliverance—
when His blessed feet shall stand in that day upon the Mount
of Olives — they will almost simultaneously be made aware of
it; for, though they may not all at once behold Him with their
eyes [why not in this day of TV?], the whole world, and nature generally, will be conscious of, and respond to, the visible
appearing and presence of the Son of God.

And the spared remnant of the dispersed of Israel, will, like
their brethren in Jerusalem, hail Him whom they crucified,
and turn to Him in true repentance.[5]

There are several psalms which are sometimes classed as
Kingdom Psalms; the seventy-second is one of them.

Give the king thy judgments, O God,
And thy righteousness unto the king's son.
He shall judge thy people with righteousness,
And the poor with justice.
The mountains shall bring peace to the people,
And the little hills, by righteousness.
He shall judge the poor of the people,
He shall save the children of the needy,
He shall break in pieces the oppressor.
They shall fear thee as long as the sun
And moon endure, through all generations.
He shall come down like rain in the mown grass;
As showers that water the earth.
In his days shall the righteous flourish;
And abundance of peace so long as the moon endureth.
He shall have dominion also from sea to sea,
And from the river unto the ends of the earth.   (vv. 1-8.)

It is "A Psalm of Solomon" but it is even greater than
Solomon in all his glory, and reaches its true fulfillment when
applied to the Messiah. It is definitely a Messianic psalm and
is so recognized by many. One of the Targums recognizes
it as such and paraphrases verse one thus:

O God, give the precepts of Thy judgment to King Messiah,
And Thy righteousness to the son of king David.

[5] David Baron, *Zechariah.*

And verse seventeen speaks, according to this paraphrase, of the pre-existence of His name:

His name shall be remembered for ever;
And before the sun existed was His name prepared;
And all the peoples shall be blessed in His merits.[6]

The kingdom depicted here goes far beyond any human kingdom in righteousness and splendor. It is universal in extent and eternal in duration. This is the kingdom for which the world yearns and waits, a kingdom with a king, yea, THE KING.

A little while and David's Son
On David's throne shall reign.

This is our hope as Christians. It is the only hope for our world. Let our prayer be:

"Come, Lord Jesus,
Come quickly."

[6] According to Talmud and Midrash, *Yinnon* — in verse 17 which is rendered *"shall be continued"*—is one of the eight names of the Messiah. Why is the Messiah named Yinnon? "Because," say the rabbis, "He will make those who sleep in the dust to flourish," i.e., He will raise the dead. A. F. Kirkpatrick, *The Psalms,* p. 417.

CHAPTER IV

MESSIANIC PROPHECY IN THE PRE-EXILIC PROPHETS
(Hosea, Joel, Amos, Obadiah, Jonah, Micah)

Hosea is the first, in order, of the Minor Prophets, as they appear in the Hebrew, Septuagint, Vulgate and Authorized Version. But it is not first in the chronological order. Hosea heads the group of the Twelve Prophets perhaps because of its size as compared with the books of the other Minor Prophets or because he is spoken of in the Talmud "as the greatest of his prophetical contemporaries" (Pesachim 87a). The name Hosea is common among the Jews. It is of the same form, in the original with the early names of Joshua (Num. 13:8) and with that of the King of Israel (II Kings 15:30). It signifies "salvation," "deliverance," which stands in marked contrast to the threatening character of his announcements. The Hebrew suggests something definite by a name as is clearly seen in the case of the promised "Hope of Israel." "Thou shalt call his name Jesus: for it is he that shall save his people from their sins" (Matt. 1:21).

Hosea has been named as the prophet of doom and destruction. This is true, but at the same time, he pointed out the way of deliverance. "O Israel, return unto the Lord thy God; for thou hast fallen by thine iniquity . . . I will heal their backsliding, I will love them freely:[1] for mine anger is turned away from him" (Hos. 14:1, 4; Heb. 5). The message which he felt he must deliver burned within him

---

[1] "Freely" — lit., "a free will gift," Nedabah, Donation, Offering, Alms.

like a flame and, like Jeremiah, he could not keep it within himself.

What must have been like a heavy burden on his heart was the fact that his people, a Covenant Nation, was divided into two rival kingdoms. His prophetic utterances were, therefore, both in the days of the kings "Uzziah, Jotham, Ahaz and Hezekiah of the house of David, as well as that of Jeroboam, the son of Joash king of Israel" (1:1). Iben Ezra[2] as well as other medieval Jewish expositors, have him prophesying during the forty years which preceded the fall of Samaria (750-720 B.C.). The book itself furnishes the evidence that this long duration was not improbable. The first prophecy in it foretells the destruction of Jehu's house, which was fulfilled in the assassination of Zechariah (II Kings 15:10). There is in it an allusion to an expedition of Shalmanezer against Israel (II Kings 10:14). This was during the reign of Hoshea, King of Israel; and if this was the first expedition against him, it must have been near the beginning of the reign of Hezekiah, King of Judah (II Kings 17:15).

The prophecies of Hosea relate mainly to Israel, the Northern Kingdom of the Ten Tribes. Reference is often made to Judah, but only incidentally.[3] The Northern Kingdom embraced the happiest regions of the country, the most fertile, as the plains of Sharon and Jezreel; the most splendidly wooded, as Ephraim, Carmel, and Lebanon and the best watered. Nature was kind to the Northland. Hence the life of the people was more joyous; and as they were far from Jerusalem, the center of the Temple, their religious life tended to deteriorate. This accounts for the religious backsliding of the kingdom of the northern part of Palestine. The charms of nature overpowered the people and they fell into

[2] Iben Ezra, *Bible Commentator* (pp. 1092-1167).
[3] Read 1:7, 11; 4:15; 5:5, 10, 14; 6:4, 11; 8:4; 11:12; 12.

the worship of idols which in turn crushed out all the
moral energy from their heart and led them into the grossest
dissoluteness of manners. "Whoredom and wine and new
wine take away the understanding" (4:11). Micah and
Isaiah rebuked the Southern Kingdom for the oppression of
the poor by the rich, for the judicial corruption, and drunkenness, but neither of them mentioned licentiousness. But in
Israel this vice in all of its ugliness had deeply penetrated
all classes. Hosea tells Israel:

THE PEOPLE

The Lord hath a controversy with the inhabitants of the land,
because there is no truth, nor mercy, nor knowledge of God in
the land. Swearing, and lying, killing and stealing, and com-
mitting adultery, they break out, and blood toucheth blood (4:
1, 2).

THE PRIESTS

My people are destroyed for lack of knowledge: because thou
hast rejected knowledge, I will also reject thee, that thou shalt
be no priest to me: seeing that thou hast forgotten the law of
thy God, I will also forget thy children. As they were increased,
so they sinned against me: therefore will I change their glory
into shame. They feed on the sin of my people, and they set
their heart on their iniquity. And there shall be like people,
like priest: and I will punish them for the wrongs they do (4:
6-9).

THE POLITICIANS

Ephraim is become like a silly dove without heart: They call
Egypt, they go to Assyria. When they shall go, I will spread
my net upon them; I will bring them down as the fowls of
the heaven. Woe to them! for they have fled from me, destruction unto them! because they have transgressed against me:
though I have redeemed them, yet they have spoken lies against
me. O Israel, thou hast destroyed thyself; but in me is thine
help. I will be thy king: where is any other that may save
thee in all thy cities? (7:11-13; 13:9, 10).

This is the picture of the internal condition of the
Northern Kingdom. The public troubles would have been
enough to make sore the heart of so tender a man as Hosea,
but he had troubles of his own to sicken him to the deep. In

the first three chapters we are told the situation. The prophet was commanded to take as a wife an impure woman, Gomer, the daughter of Diblaim, who bore him three children. The impurity of the woman points to the idolatry of the land, and the names of the children[4] have a symbolical reference to Jehovah's relation to the people of Israel. In the Old Testament, the covenant relation between Jehovah and Israel is represented as a marriage (Jer. 2:2). Consequently, Israel's idolatry and apostasy are symbolically designated as adultery. They had apostatized; therefore He would no longer favor them, not look upon them as His people. Another symbolical action, the command to Hosea to take his erring wife back, recorded in chapter three, intimated that the children of Israel, as punishment of their adultery, should be deprived of their independence and

> abide many days without a king and without a prince, and without a sacrifice and without an image, and without an ephod, and without teraphim: Afterward shall the children of Israel return, and seek the Lord their God, and David their king; and shall fear the Lord and his goodness in the latter days (3:4, 5).[5]

The great aim of Hosea was to bring the Ten Tribes to repentance, to induce them to forsake their idols and return to Jehovah. The passage just cited emphasizes the love that God has for His people Israel notwithstanding her unfaithfulness, "a love which is punitive and yet restorative." Hosea gives several fine pictures of the restoration, graphically depicting the grief of the Father's heart and the resulting restoration:

> Thy calf, O Samaria, is cast off;
> Mine anger is kindled against them . . .

[4] *Jezreel*: "God sows," as well as "scatters" (see Jer. 31:10; Zech. 10:9).
Lo-ruhamah: "Not beloved," the unpitied one.
Lo-ammi: "Not My people," Israel rejected.
[5] *"In the latter days"*: The Messianic era is usually described in this Hebrew expression.

A craftsman made it: it is not God.
Yea, the calf of Samaria shall be broken in shivers.
(8:5, 6 — A.J.T.)

How shall I give thee up, Ephraim?
How shall I surrender thee, Israel?
How shall I make thee as Admah?
How shall I set thee as Zebohim?
My heart is turned within me,
My compassions are kindled together.   (11:8 — A.R.V.)

How is Israel to come back to God? One of the psalmists
had this in mind when he asked:

If thou, Lord, shouldest mark iniquities,
O Lord, who shall stand?
But there is forgiveness with thee,
That thou mayest be feared.

Let Israel hope in the Lord:
For with the Lord there is mercy,
And with him is plenteous redemption.
And he shall redeem Israel
From all his iniquities.   (Ps. 130:3, 4, 7, 8.)

Love, according to Hosea, is the center of God's great
plan of salvation. The Good Shepherd is out in search of the
lost lamb:

Behold, I will allure her,
And bring her to the wilderness,
And speak comfortably unto her (hearth).
And I will give her vineyards there,
And the valley of Achor for a door of hope.
And she shall respond there as in the days of her youth,
When she came out of the land of Egypt.
And it shall be at that day, saith Jehovah,
That thou shalt call me Ishi [my husband]
And shall call no more Baali [my Baal] . . .
And I will betroth thee unto me forever;
Yea, I will betroth thee unto me in righteousness and justice,
And with loving-kindness and mercies.
And I will even betroth thee unto me in faithfulness,
And thou shalt know Jehovah.   (2:14-16, 19, 20.)

Hosea has much to offer in connection with God's plan of salvation for the whole world which, of course, includes Israel. The many Messianic allusions are, therefore, of vital importance. Compare Matthew 2:15 with Hosea 11:1; Matthew 9:13 and 12:7, with Hosea 6:6; Romans 9:25,26, with Hosea 2:23; and I Corinthians 15:55, with Hosea 13:14.

These passages have been considered Messianic by many of the great commentators of all time, including some of the rabbis of Talmudic Era. They may not have been considered directly Messianic, in the strictest sense of the word; but they contain promises relating to Messianic times, in which they receive their fulfillment. Their peculiarity, according to Hengstenberg in his *Christ in the Old Testament*, Vol. I, p. 182, "as compared with those of the time of David and Solomon, consists in · the connection of the promise with threatenings of judgments, and in the Messiah's appearing as the light of those who walk in the deepest darkness of the divine judgments." These promises supported God's people in the midst of the gloom and darkness of the times. "I will heal their backsliding, I will love them freely: for mine anger is turned away from him. I will be as the dew unto Israel; he shall grow as the lily, and cast forth his roots as Lebanon" (Hos. 14:4,5).

JOEL

The second book of the Minor Prophets is that of Joel, son of Pethuel. The name Joel is not uncommon among the Jews. It appears as early as the time of Samuel (I Sam. 8:2), survives through the centuries till we reach the days of Nehemiah (Neh. 11:9) unto our own times. The name, like most Hebrew names, is significant. It means "Jehovah is God." Little is known of the personal life of the prophet other than that he is a native of Judah. He speaks of Zion seven times, of Judah and Jerusalem six times and thrice does he speak of the children and Jerusalem, in a way that leaves no doubt upon this point.

The date of Joel's prophecy is one of the most debated problems in the field of Biblical criticism. Dr. Joseph Klausner, in his recently published book says:

> His beautiful style and his position in the Scriptures between Hosea and Amos caused the ancient interpreters to think that he was one of the earlier prophets; the fact that he mentions no king at all, but on the contrary that the priests and the "ministers of the altar" are mentioned three times (1:9, 13; 2:17), gave rise to the idea that Joel was the earliest of the prophets, prophesying in the time of the son of Amaziah, king of Judah (836-796 B.C.), who became king at seven years of age, Jehoiada the priest ruling the land until the king came of age.[6]

Dr. Klausner refuses to place Joel after Hosea and places him instead at the side of Malachi (490-475 B.C.), contrary to the fact that "tradition as well as most of the Jewish commentators favour the early date,"[7] which leads us to accept the view held by Merrill F. Unger, Ph. D., who in his *Introductory Guide to the Old Testament*, says: "Its spirit and style are unlike the post-exilic prophets, Haggai, Zachariah and Malachi, and clearly belong to the period of Hebrew classical literature."[8]

The book naturally falls into two main parts. In the first Joel speaks, and in the second, Jehovah. The prophet first describes a double scourge of locusts and drought (1:1-2:17), together with a call to repentance. He sees in this attack an emblem of a more terrible attack by swarms of heathen soldiers in his day as well as in the last days yet to come and he calls upon all classes to lament and to mourn over the desolation of the land. The prophet himself cries to Jehovah on behalf of his own brethren. The second portion of the book (2:18-3:21), has promises — reparation for the damage of the plague, rich blessing "unto His people," judgment and destruction upon their enemies. This of course has given rise to much criticism, especially among those who

[6] *The Messianic Idea in Israel*, p. 206.
[7] Rabbi Dr. S. M. Lehrman, *Joel*, p. 57.
[8] M. F. Unger, *Introductory Guide to the Old Testament*, p. 337 (Zondervan Publishing House, Grand Rapids, Mich.).

would have Joel in the post-exilic period and who hold the first part as an allegory and the locusts representing nations. But it need not be so. We know that God used real locusts in punishing Egypt (Ex. 10:12). Locusts are threatened as an instrument of future punishment (Deut. 28:38) while Solomon in his prayer mentions locusts as a scourge among many of the other plagues that may come to the land and people (I Kings 8:37). The prophet refers to a visitation of real and actual locusts, which are at the same time, types of still further scourges. In the light of the literal interpretation, we find three predictions:

1. The plague of locusts and drought, and the removal of that plague (1:4; 2:25).

2. The effusion of the Holy Spirit, typified by the refreshing rain which brought life back to the fields (2:21-23, 28-32).

3. The day of judgment, typified by the destruction of the locusts and the reign of righteousness accompanying and following the judgment (ch. 3).

It is generally admitted that Joel stood near the beginning of written prophecy and held the position of a type, or model, to the prophets that followed, such as Amos, Hosea, Micah and Isaiah. He was one of God's noblemen, a prophet sent from God, with a well laid out plan for the redemption of man and the establishing of His Kingdom. In this, Israel was to have a part: "And I will bless them that bless thee, and curse him that curseth thee; and in thee shall *all the families* of the earth be blessed" (Gen. 12:3).

The basis of the hope of Israel's future and glorious destiny for mankind was the coming of the Messiah. Joel does not describe or mention the Messiah but speaks only of the advent of Jehovah and thus illustrates the fact that there are two lines of prophecy running through the Old Testament — one presenting redemption as wrought by a human redeemer, the "Seed of the woman" (Gen. 3:15), of Semitic stock (Gen. 9:26), of the Patriarchs (Gen. 12:1-3; 49:10), of David

(II Sam. 7:12), the child of the virgin (Isa. 7:14), the Divine King (Isa. 9:6,7) who is also the Suffering Servant (Isa. 53). The other line of prophecy presents redemption wrought by a divine redeemer, Jehovah Himself coming down to his earth to set up His Kingdom in Zion. This is the line of prophecy too often overlooked and little understood. This is the Gospel preached by Joel:

> Be glad then ye children of Zion, and rejoice in the Lord your God, for he hath given you the former rain moderately, and he will cause to come down for you the rain, the former rain and the latter rain the first month (2:23).[9]

Hengstenberg renders this verse more correctly and in agreement with Targum Jonathan, the Vulgate, Rashi and Iben Ezra: "And ye sons of Zion, exult and rejoice in Jehovah your God; for He giveth you the *Teacher of righteousness*, and he poureth down upon you rain, the former rain and the latter rain, for the first time." And observe,

> There can be only the choice between Messiah as the long promised Teacher and the *ideal* teacher — the collective body of all divine teachers. That we have not here before us an ordinary collective body is shown by the parallel passage in Isaiah, according to which the glory of the Lord is manifested in the teacher.[10]

But we must not overlook the fact that the future blessing of God's people in the Book of Joel refers to the Messianic Age. He speaks of "the great and terrible day of the Lord," which will be "a day of darkness and of gloominess, a day of clouds and of thick darkness. . . . And the Lord shall utter his voice before his army for his camp is very great: for he is strong that executeth his word: for the day of the Lord is great and very terrible; and who can abide it?" (2:2,11) But the day of the Lord will come a second time:

> And it shall come to pass afterward, that I will pour out my spirit upon all flesh; and your sons and your daughters shall

---

[9] *Former rain*: Heb. H'moreh L'zedakah. Rashi and Iben Ezra interpret the word as teacher. See II Kings 17:28; Job 36:22; Isaiah 9:15; 30:20 where the word *moreh* is so translated.
[10] Hengstenberg's *Christology of the Old Testament*, Vol. 1, pp. 325, 326.

prophesy, your old men shall dream dreams, your young men shall see visions: And also upon the servants and upon the handmaids in those days I will pour out my Spirit. And I will show wonders in the heavens and in the earth, and fire and pillars of smoke. The sun shall be turned into darkness, and the moon into blood, before the great and terrible day of the Lord come. And it shall come to pass, that whosoever shall call on the name of the Lord shall be delivered: for in the mount of Zion and in Jerusalem shall be deliverance, as the Lord hath said, and in the remnant whom the Lord shall call. (2:28-32; see Heb. 3:1-5.)

Who is it that pours out the Holy Spirit? It is true that Christ in His prayer (John 14:16) asks the Father to send the Comforter, and a little further on (John 14:26) He says that HE will send Him. Elsewhere our Lord tells His disciples that He is the one who baptizes with the Holy Ghost (Matt. 3:11). The promise of the outpouring of the Holy Spirit in this Book of Joel was fulfilled on the day of Pentecost (Acts 2:16), but this great prophecy was not exhausted in that great experience of the early followers of our Lord. "The miracle of Pentecost ushered in a new dispensation to which Joel had pointed, and on which his words are to receive an ever-increasing fulfillment."[11]

Peter interprets the advent of the Spirit (Acts 2:14-36) as the fulfillment of the prophecy of Joel, which predicted the advent of the divine Spirit in the last days upon all classes and conditions of men. Joel's prophecy is one of a series of predictions of the coming of the Spirit. Says C. H. C. MacGregor:

> The story of the Book of Joel is the story with a national bearing. The language of the book had a clear and definite meaning for those to whom it was spoken, and no doubt much of it had already been fulfilled. But the fulfillment of the book as a whole belongs to the time of the millennial glory when Israel shall have received and enthroned as King the long rejected Messiah.[12]

[11] A. F. Kirkpatrick, *The Doctrine of the Prophets*, p. 75.
[12] *Messages of the Old Testament.*

Amos

According to a probable derivation, Amos means *burden,
or burdensome,*[13] which fits in perfectly with the prophecies
he uttered concerning the ten tribes, Judah, and the nations
surrounding Palestine. The rabbis saw in his name an indica-
tion of some bodily defect, resembling Moses, who was heavy
in speech.[14] Amos was born in a little village, Tekoa which
was in the hill country of Judah, about twelve miles south of
Jerusalem and six miles to the south of Bethlehem of Judea.
In his answer to Amaziah, the priest of Bethel, he says that
he was a herdman and a gatherer of sycamore fruit, and
before this he laid emphasis on the fact that he "was no
prophet, neither was I a prophet's son" (1:1; 7:14, 15), by
which he wanted him to understand that he did not belong
to the "order" of prophets, not even the disciple of any prophet,
as was Elisha who followed Elijah and in due time became
his successor. We meet here with one of God's great messengers who without previous special training was called from the
flock and farm to the important office of prophet.

But we must not allow ourselves to think that Amos was
an *Am Ha-Arez,* an ignoramus.[15] The book before us, though
only of nine chapters furnishes abundant evidence that he
was a "man of letters" and well qualified for presenting
this literary masterpiece. Of him Dr. Driver says, "His language is pure, his style classical and refined, his thought is
often finely expressed."

Amos prophesied "in the days of Uzziah, King of Judah, and

[13] In Psalm 68:19—"who daily loadeth us" and in the R.V., "who daily
beareth our burden," or as the Targum has it, "who daily beareth us" and
in Isaiah 46:3, 4, the same word (H'hamusim) is used in the phrase, "O
house of Jacob . . . that are borne by me" justify our naming Amos to mean
burden, or burdensome.

[14] Lev. R. s. 10 begins with "I sent Amos, and they named him stammerer"
(psillos, one unable to pronounce certain letters, stammerer; Yalk. Is. 307
v. Amos).

[15] *Am Ha-Arez.* The literal meaning of the term "people of the land."
Its connotation, we are told, is derived from the fact that those who lived
on the land had little by way of education or accomplishments and therefore
could not occupy positions of importance in the Jewish community.

in the days of Jeroboam, the son of Joash, King of Israel two years before the earthquake" (1:1). On comparing II Kings 14:2, 17, 23 and 15:1, we infer that Amos prophesied in the latter half of the reign of Jeroboam II, who ruled from 787 to 747 B.C. The reign of Jeroboam II was one of outward prosperity and brilliancy. His father Joash had left him a kingdom greatly strengthened since the days of the depression in the days of Jehoahaz. But it was left for Jeroboam still further to extend the limits of the kingdom of Israel. It seemed that the royal magnificence of David and Solomon had returned, but the internal condition of the kingdom was that of corruption and decay. The country was ruined by prosperity. Rich from the spoils of war and the profits of commerce, the people gave way to luxury and all its vices. Drunkenness and sensuality spread on every side. Public festival and private feasts were the scenes of revolting excesses. There was everywhere lying, stealing, murder, and even the sacred places were not free from the corruption of the times. The calf-worship at Bethel and Dan had taken the place of the simple form of worship. Love of virtue and knowledge of God had vanished from the land.

It was in such a state of affairs that Amos was called to prophesy and his ministry was undoubtedly effective. The high priest Amaziah did not like it. He sent a complaint to the king, and here is what he said: "Amos hath conspired against thee in the midst of the house of Israel: the land is not able to bear all his words. For thus Amos saith, Jeroboam shall die by the sword, and Israel shall surely be led away captive out of their own land" (7:10, 11).

Turning to Amos, the high priest says: "O thou seer, go flee away into the land of Judah, and eat bread and prophesy there, but prophesy not again in Bethel: for it is the king's chapel and it is the royal court" (7:12, 13).

Says Professor John Paterson,

The King James Version is much too polite here and does more than justice to Amaziah. The high ecclesiastical dignitary was positively rude. "Get out!" he screams, "preach elsewhere where you really belong." Amaziah classes Amos with people with whom Amos refused to be classed: the professional preachers of that time whose only thought was cheap notoriety and the fee they expected to receive.[16]

Amos, the true prophet of God, was not that type of man. Nor was he frightened by threats, for we hear him say:

> Thou sayest, prophesy not against Israel, and drop not a word against the house of Isaac. Therefore thus saith the Lord, thy wife shall be an harlot in the city, and thy sons and thy daughters shall fall by the sword, and thy land shall be divided by line; and thou shalt die in an unclean land, and Israel shall surely go forth into captivity from his land (7:16, 17).

Amos had a stern message for that pleasure-seeking age. He was the prophet of woe, but he also had a message of hope.

The Book of Amos is divided into three parts: The first, from chapter 1:1 to 2:16, is made up of judgments upon surrounding nations including Judah and Israel; the second, from chapter 3:1 to 9:10, consists of Jehovah's indictment of the whole family of Jacob; and third, chapter 9:11-15, the promise of blessing to restored Israel in and through the Messiah.

Because the people of Judah despised Jehovah's law, and allowed themselves to be enticed into idolatry, fire was to be sent upon them "to devour the places of Jerusalem" (2:4, 5). The overthrow of Israel is certain, but the house of Jacob is not to be utterly destroyed (9:8). "In that day"— after judgment had come to the sinful kingdom, and the house of Israel had been sifted among all nations — "will I raise up the tabernacle (sukkah) of David that hath fallen, and close up the breaches thereof; and I will raise up his ruins, and I will build it as in the days of old" (9:11). Moreover, just as on "the day of the Lord," the day ordained for punishment, the order of nature will be changed for the worse, so in the time of the Messianic reign it will be changed for the better:

---

[16] *The Goodly Fellowship of the Prophets,* pp. 19, 20 (Scribners).

> Behold, the days come, saith the Lord, the plowman shall
> overtake the reaper, and the treader of grapes him that soweth
> seed; and mountains shall drop sweet wine, and all the hills
> shall melt. And I will turn the captivity of my people Israel,
> and they shall build the waste cities, and inhabit them; and
> they shall plant vineyards, and drink the wine thereof; they
> shall also make gardens, and eat the fruit of them, And I will
> plant them upon their land, and they shall no more be plucked
> up out of their land which I have given them, saith the Lord
> thy God (9:13-15.

Surely such a thorough revival of all things could only be
fulfilled in the risen Christ! In Him the destinies of Israel and
the world find their goal. The revival was not fulfilled by the
return from the Babylonian captivity, under Zerubbabel and
Ezra. Israel was not then planted in the land to dwell forever;
and the Tabernacle of David, which had fallen down, was
not then set up. The raising of the Tabernacle of David
commenced with the coming of Christ, the founding of the
Church by His disciples, the gathering together of all nations
upon whom the Lord reveals His name and the final ingather-
ing of both Jewish and Gentile believers under the canopy
of God's saving grace. With this agree the words of the
apostle James (Acts 15:13-17). It is also the order of Romans
11:24-27 and is in accord with some of the ancient rabbis.
Thus, in Sanhedrin 96 b, where the Messiah is called the
"Son of the Fallen," the name is explained by a reference
to Amos 9:11. In Bereshith Rab. 88, after enumerating the
unexpected deliverances which Israel had formerly experienced,
it continues: "Who could have expected that the fallen
Tabernacle of David should be raised up by God, as it is
written (Amos 9:11) and who should have expected that
the whole world should become one bundle" (be gathered into
one Church).[17]

---

[17] Edersheim, *Life and Times of Jesus*, Vol. II; Bereshith Rabba and Midrash on Genesis, dating in its present form from about the sixth century.

OBADIAH

Concerning the personal life of Obadiah, a "Servant of the Lord," nothing is known. A statement in the Talmud identifies him with the Obadiah who lived in the reign of Ahab (I Kings 18:3-16) and thus places him during the reign of Jehoram son of Jehoshaphat, king of Judah (848-842 B.C.). At that time the Philistines and Arabians overran Judah and plundered Jerusalem, and the Edomites who were long time enemies of Judah revealed their never ceasing hatred against them.[18] These historical events meet all the demands of the prophecy and explain why Edom has remained to this day a type of all oppressors and persecutors of Jews.

Edom is here, as in the prophecy of Isaiah (43:1-6), a symbol of the enemies of God. Obadiah sets forth a strong denunciation of the Edomites for their haughty and arrogant spirit, and for the evils which they had brought upon the people of God.

> In the day when thou stoodest on the other side,
> In the day when strangers carried off his substance,
> When foreigners entered his gates
> And cast lots upon Jerusalem,
> Even thou wast one of them! (v. 11).
>
> For the violence done to thy brother Jacob
> Shame shall cover thee, and thou shalt be cut off for ever.
> (v. 10.)

The little prophecy of twenty-one verses is full of warnings of severe punishments. "The judgment of God upon Edom is poetic justice," says Dr. G. Campbell Morgan: "As thou hast done, it shall be done unto thee." The New Testament states it thus: "Be not deceived; God is not mocked: for whatsoever a man soweth, that shall he also reap" (Gal. 6:7). That is the story of Edom who in the day of the destruction of Jerusalem by the Chaldeans, cried "Rase it, rase it" (Ps. 137:7). For this pride and cruel hatred the total destruction of Edom was decreed (vv. 3, 4, 10) and five years

---

[18] See II Kings 8:20-22; II Chronicles 21:8-20; Joel 3:3-6; Amos 1:6.

after the destruction of Jerusalem, Nebuchadnezzer crushed the Edomites.

Obadiah occupies an important place in God's plan of salvation. It serves to emphasize that fact that the Lord will indeed punish those who oppose His own chosen people. At the same time it closes with the promise of deliverance for Zion. The single Messianic prophecy is that of verse twenty-one: "And saviours shall come up on Mount Zion, to judge the mount of Esau; and the kingdom shall be the Lord's."

This message is one of strength and comfort to those who are the Lord's.

JONAH

The Book of Jonah contains an account of certain events which have taken place in the life and experience of a prophet called Jonah. This prophet is a historical person who lived during the reign of Jeroboam II, that is, during the eighth century (782-753 B. C.) and it is generally agreed that he is to be identified as the author of the book. This is what II Kings has to say on this subject:

> He [Jeroboam] restored the border of Israel from the entering of Hammath unto the sea of the plain, according to the word of the Lord God of Israel, which he spake by the hand of his servant Jonah, the son of Amittai, the prophet, which was of Gath-hepher (II Kings 14:25).

This passage and his mission to Nineveh are the only records that we have of his prophetic activity. Is he the author of the book which has come down to us under his name? Jewish tradition says that he is, and for this reason it was placed in the Old Testament Canon among the prophets. Moreover, to this day, the Book of Jonah is read in its entirety during the afternoon service on the Day of Atonement (Yom Kippur), as the Haftorah, the prophetic reading after the reading of the Law (Sidroh).[19]

---

[19] It is believed that the reading of the Haftorah was introduced in 168 B.C. instead of the Scripture reading prohibited under the decree of Antiochus Epiphanes. Another reason why we read the Book of Jonah is because it informs us that God pardons and forgives those who repent, and that God extends his compassions over all that he has created.

There is nothing in the style of the book at variance with the idea that Jonah wrote it. The genuine historical character of the book has been defended by such scholars as Piper, Luedervald, Hengstenberg and Delitzsch. Wrote Professor Harper:

> The historical character of the Book of Jonah is not to be rejected: (1) because it contains but few of those historical particulars which are commonly regarded as necessary for authentification; or (2) because of a supposed superabundance of the miraculous element in the book; or (3) because the apparent improbability, as we may regard the event, of Nineveh's repentance; or (4) because Jonah's conduct as exhibited in the book seems incredible. These objections disappear, when we consider the narrative in the light of revelation and of history.[20]

The main question, therefore, is not that which relates to the historical contents of the Book of Jonah only, but that which relates to its aim. It contains no prediction of a direct Christian import. Its subject is Nineveh. Jonah was, however, in his own person a type and a prophetic sign of Christ. The miracle of his deliverance from the belly of the fish was a type of Christ's Resurrection.

Two incidents in the Book of Jonah are cited by Jesus in such a way as to lead us to conclude that He believed that they had occurred. One is the existing of Jonah in the belly of the fish for three days; and the other, the repentance of the men of Nineveh at the preaching of Jonah. The New Testament record is clear:

One day, on the shores of the Lake of Galilee, where Jesus was teaching the multitudes that followed Him; speaking as never man spoke, and healing all manner of diseases and sicknesses, enabling the lame to walk, the blind to see and the deaf to hear;

> certain of the scribes and of the Pharisees answered, saying: Master, we would see a sign from thee. But He answered and said unto them, An evil and adulterous generation seeketh a

sign; and there shall no sign be given to it, but the sign of the prophet Jonas: For as Jonas was three days and three nights in the whale's belly; so shall the Son of man be three days and three nights in the heart of the earth. The men of Nineveh shall rise in judgment with this generation, and shall condemn it: because they repented at the preaching of Jonas; and, behold, a greater than Jonas is here (Matt. 12:38-41).

This settles the matter. We have here Christ's approval of both Jonah and his book, and this, please note, does not place Him among those who were ignorant. Jesus was not ignorant. This was the Son of God "speaking that which He knew, and testifying to that which He had seen," having before Him the vision of the past and future alike and knowledge of nature's secrets and the secrets of the underworld. We can say with thanksgiving: Lord, Thou knowest all things!

It is because the message of Jonah means things of depth and sacredness, that Professor Cornill wrote:

I have read the Book of Jonah at least a hundred times, and I will publicly avow, for I am not ashamed of my weakness, that I cannot even now take up this marvelous book, nay, not even speak of it, without the tears rising to my eyes and my heart beating higher. . . . This book is one of the deepest and grandest that was ever written, and I should like to say to every one who approaches it, "Take off thy shoes from off thy feet, for the place whereon thou standest is holy ground."

MICAH

Micah the Morashite was a contemporary of Isaiah as well as Hosea and exercised the ministry during the reigns of Jotham, Ahaz and Hezekiah. This we learn from the opening verse of the book which bears his name and also from Jeremiah (26:18). He is vigorous and fearless in denunciation of wrong. He describes the moral corruption of his times and arraigns the political and religious rulers as the leaders in sin:

Hear this, I pray you, ye heads of the house of Jacob, and rulers of the house of Israel, that abhor judgment, and pervert all equity. That build up Zion with blood, and Jerusalem with iniquity. The heads thereof judge for reward, and the priests

> thereof teach for hire, and the prophets thereof divine for money: Yet will they lean upon Jehovah, and say: Is not the Lord in the midst of us? No evil shall come upon us (Mic. 3:9-11).

Concerning his right to speak the prophet does not leave us in any doubt. He reveals the source of his fearless denunciation of wrong, when he says: "But as for me, I am full of power by the Spirit of Jehovah, and of judgment, and of might, to declare unto Jacob his transgression, and to Israel his sin" (Mic. 3:8). He makes it clear that there is a difference between the profession prophets and the true prophet of God:

> Concerning the prophets that make my people err, that cry: Peace, when their teeth have anything to bite; and whoso putteth not into their mouths, they even prepare war against him. Therefore night shall be unto you, that ye shall not have a vision; and it shall be dark unto you that ye shall not divine (Mic. 3:5, 6).

The prophet's burning words against the authorities of state, who failed to take action to prevent injustices and who even shared in the proceeds (Mic. 3:1-4, 9-11), and his attack on the so-called religious leaders whom he called "hirelings" — brought forth a spiritual awakening in the heart and conscience of King Hezekiah who prayed to Jehovah for forgiveness (Jer. 26:17-19).

The best-known passages in the Book of Micah are the resplendent visions of things to come. Chapter 4:1-3 is the general announcement of future salvation and blessing, which the presence of the Messiah will introduce. This is "a vision, not of the near or foreseeable future," says Rabbi S. Goldman, "but of the end of days, i.e., of the Messianic age."[21] It is an event toward which the whole creation moves, though it still seems so far, and is constantly ignored in our day. This truth is of ultimate importance for the future of the world, namely, the acceptance by the nations of God's way of life:

[21] *Micah* (Soncino Press, London).

> And many nations shall come and say, Come, and let us go up to the mountain of the Lord, and to the house of the God of Jacob; and he will teach us his ways, and we will walk in his paths: for the law shall go forth of Zion, and the word of the Lord from Jerusalem (Mic. 4:2).

Then abruptly the prophet introduces the One who will usher in that glorious, longed-for Messianic Age, the remarkable prophecy of the birth of the promised Messiah in Bethlehem of Judah:

> But thou, Bethlehem Ephratah, though thou be little among the thousands of Judah, yet out of thee shall come forth unto me that is to be ruler in Israel; whose goings forth have been from of old, from everlasting[22] (Mic. 5:2; Heb. 5:1).

Of course this prophetic statement is a stumbling block to all who would limit God's prophets to their time and environment (and they would push it up or down to suit themselves), and as we might expect, non-Messianic interpretations have been given. In this, as in many other instances, the Messianic interpretation here is old. Says A. Lukyn Williams, D.D.,

> Only a very jejune system of interpretation can refer these words to the short period of three hundred years from Micah to David, and it is little better to explain them of the time from the future birth of the Messiah back to David, or to suppose that His long existence was only in the thought and purpose of God. It is not easy to get over the impression that Micah's language implies the expectation of the coming of a Divine Person who has existed from eternity.[23]

"Little town of Bethlehem!" At the time of our Saviour's birth men quoted part of Micah's prophecy about Bethlehem of Judea. Thank God, we are still quoting that little town that has become the best-known place in all the world.

Micah, one of a galaxy of the true prophets of God, was

[22] Dr. C. I. Scofield is correct in stating in a footnote: "The child was born in Bethlehem, but the Son was from everlasting" (Scofield Bible, page 949). *From ancient of days*: We are told in the Talmud that the name of the Messiah is included among the seven things created before the world was brought into being (P'sachim Fol. 54, col. 1). In Proverbs 8:22, 23, Wisdom is personified and is spoken of as existing before "ever the earth was," and is in the same sense used here.

[23] *The Hebrew Christian Messiah*, p. 27.

one with them in their expression and hope concerning the coming of the promised Saviour of men and of a time when—

> . . . they shall beat their swords into plowshares, and their spears into pruninghooks: nation shall not lift up a sword against nation, neither shall they learn war any more. But they shall sit every man under his vine and under his fig tree; and none shall make them afraid (Mic. 4:3, 4).

Then the Messiah will be Israel's Shepherd, who will re-gather His earthly people and feed them so that they will be satisfied and with one voice they will display His grace:

> Who is a God like unto thee, that pardoneth iniquity, and passeth by the transgression of the remnant of his heritage?
>
> He retaineth not his anger for ever, because he delighted in mercy. He will turn again, he will have compassion upon us; he will subdue our iniquities; and thou wilt cast all their sins into the depths of the sea. Thou wilt perform the truth to Jacob, and the mercy to Abraham, which thou hast sworn unto our fathers from the days of old (Mic. 7:18-20).

This our Lord Jesus will do when He returns to claim the throne of David and to reign over all the earth. "And so all Israel shall be saved" (Rom. 11:26, 27). Oh, what a day of rejoicing that will be!

CHAPTER V

MESSIANIC PROPHECY IN ISAIAH

Someone suggested that "Messianic prophecy is all prophecy that refers, whether more or less distinctly, to the coming of Christ, to His work of salvation, and to the growth and consummation of His kingdom."

Broadly viewed, therefore, the whole Old Testament is Messianic; as the whole history of Israel was but a preparation for the incarnation. Israel's history has no significance except as a preparation for the coming of the Messiah. As a nation Israel resisted the Holy Spirit. Nevertheless that history was so shaped by divine patience that every portion of it was pedagogic and digested to lead to the One who became "the desire of all nations" and the "Hope of Israel." From Genesis to Malachi the single aim of the Old Testament was to impress upon the national mind the need and the nature of the Saviour and the certainty of His coming. Every brave leader, like Joshua, became a type of the great "Captain of our salvation"; every prophet a type of the "Teacher come from God"; every sufferer like Job or Jeremiah, a type of "the Man of sorrows," every victorious king, like David, a type of "the King of glory." Whatever was sublime in pain or triumph was immortalized in literature only that it might be ready to interpret the life and ministry of *Immanuel.*

In the Book of Isaiah we find the pictures of the coming Messiah most vividly portrayed. As we read this book we cannot but feel that here is a prophet who was admitted to closer, a more inward and spiritual, fellowship with God than any of his brethren. He knew more of His mind, and more of

His spirit, rose to a larger prevision of "the grace and truth" which "came to Jesus Christ." That is what we mean when we call him "the Evangel" of the Old Testament. He had seen God face to face. His was the vision of "the Lord sitting upon a throne, high and lifted up," which made him a prophet (Isa. 6:1-8). What he had seen, others might see, and it was his ruling task and the endeavor of his life to make them see it.

The promise in Isaiah, chapter seven, is blended with several other passages in the book known as the "Immanuel Passages." These are: Isaiah 7:13-17; 9:6,7; 11:1-9, and have been declared by scholars as Messianic.

It was in 735 B.C. when Assyria threatened Syria, Israel, and Judah. In an invasion, Syria would suffer the first attack; and Syria and Israel, closely connected, found themselves in sore straits. If Assyria should attack them in front, there was Judah, their enemy, in the rear. Since Assyria's coming was certain, Syria and Israel united to force Judah into a triple alliance. Ahaz, Judah's king, thought otherwise, and arranged plans to make terms directly with Assyria and thus avoid the danger of invasion. To force the alliance with Judah, Syria and Israel declared war and laid siege to Jerusalem. It was at that time that Isaiah appeared on the scene with a special message from Jehovah. To Ahaz he said, "Be calm and quiet, have faith in Jehovah, all will be well" (Isa. 7:3-9). How Ahaz received this message we learn indirectly from the record. He was deaf to the words of the prophet. Soon after, Isaiah pays the king another visit in order to persuade him of the truth of the message sent from God. "Ahaz," said Isaiah, "you would not believe my former message from Jehovah; here I come again. Let me give you a sign and let it be the evidence of this truth; ask it either in the depth, or in the height above." But Ahaz said, "I will not ask (a sign) neither will I tempt the Lord" (Isa. 7:10-12).

The prophet, freed from all responsibility and restraint, utters the passage under consideration:

> Hear ye now, O house of David: is it a small thing for you to weary men, that ye will weary my God also? Therefore the Lord Himself shall give you a sign, behold a virgin shall conceive, and bear a son, and shall call his name Immanuel (Isa. 7:13, 14).

The word Immanuel appears here for the first time. It means "God with us" and is prophetic for "that day," when God would manifest Himself to and among His people, for their salvation and the consummation of His Kingdom. How is that kingdom to come? "Behold a virgin shall conceive . . ."

There are two principal arguments against the Messianic application of this prophecy:

1. That the term "the virgin" (h'alma) does not strictly mean "virgin," that in that case the term bethulah should have been used.

2. That the foretelling of the birth of a child centuries after the delivery of the prophecy could have conveyed no proof to Ahaz who was in need of some tangible evidence that the designs of his enemies would be frustrated. These arguments are regarded by the critics as unanswerable. Let us see whether this is really the case.

In most instances where doubt exists as to the proper rendering of a word, the etymology will generally be found as a safe guide in arriving at the true meaning. There are, however, many words in the Old Testament of which the root has become obsolete. Whenever such is the case, it is necessary to examine in what sense such words are used in other places where they occur. Alma is one of those words whose derivation seems to be doubtful, at least about which lexicographers and commentators do not agree. There are many who derive the term alma from the ordinary verb olam, to hide, to conceal — the secluded one; for virgins, they say, were kept in strict seclusion from the company of men in accordance with the custom of Eastern nations. Hence the author of the Book of Maccabees speaks of "the virgins that are shut up" (II Macc. 3:19), and Philo tells of "virgins that are kept in chambers." Jerome, who studied Hebrew under Jewish rabbis around A. D. 400, thought it possible to render *alma* by *virgo* in Genesis 24:43 and Isaiah 7:14. It should not be forgotten that the "seventy" (LXX) Jewish pre-Christian translators of Genesis (280 B. C.), and of Isaiah (200 B.C.) presumed that their rendering of *alma* by *parthenos* in Genesis 24:43 and Isaiah 7:14 was in their mind a justifiable rendering. "So far as we have any evidence," says Dr. Robert Dick Wilson, "the citation of Isaiah 7:14 in Matthew 1:23 is thus justified by the Jewish interpretation up to the time when Matthew was written" ("Notes and Notices," *The Princeton Theological Review*).

Modern higher critics and Jewish antagonists maintain that if a virgin was meant, the term *bethula* would have been used and not *alma*. Let us see whether this argument is sustained by the use of these terms in the Old Testament. The word *alma* occurs at least seven times in the Old Testament and it is translated as follows:

A. Genesis 24:43: "Behold, I stand by the well of water; and it shall come to pass, that when the virgin (*h'alma*) cometh forth to draw water, and I say to her, Give me, I pray thee, a little water from the pitcher to drink." In our A.V. it is rendered "virgin," and in the Revised Version by "the maiden." Targum Onkelos '*ulemta*; LXX, *parthenos*; Jerome, *virgo*.

B. Exodus 2:8: "And Pharaoh's daughter said to her, Go. And the maid (*h'alma*) went and called the child's mother." Both the Authorized and Revised Versions render *alma* "*maiden*." According to most Jewish commentators and Josephus, the "maiden" here alluded to was Miriam who about that time was ten or twelve years old.

C. Proverbs 30:19: "The way of an eagle in the air; the way of a serpent upon a rock; the way of a ship in the midst of the sea; and the way of a man with a maid" (*alma*). Here the allusion is evidently to a pure maiden and is expressly stated as different from the way of the adulterous woman. The force in this case seems to depend upon the *alma* being considered as a virgin. The Targum reads *ulemta*.

D. Song of Solomon 1:3: "Because of the savour of thy good ointments thy name is as ointment poured forth, therefore do the virgins (*Alomoth*) love thee."

E. Song of Solomon 6:8: "There are three score queens, and fourscore concubines, and virgins (*Alomoth*) without number." These verses may be explained as meaning that the *alomoth* as inhabitants of the harem are distinct from the queens (wives) and the concubines, and are shown here as applied to the virgins.

F. Psalm 68:25: "The singers went before, the players on instruments followed after; among them were the damsels (*Alomoth*) playing with timbrels."

G. Isaiah 7:14: "Therefore the Lord Himself shall give you a sign; Behold, the virgin (*h'alma*) shall conceive, and bear a son, and shall call his name Immanuel."

From the above we may conclude with a quotation from the Hebrew scholar, Dr. Robert D. Wilson:

> The word *alma,* so far as known, never meant "young married woman"; and secondly since the presumption in common law and usage was, and is, that every *alma* is a virgin and virtuous, until she is proven not to be, we have a right to assume that Rebecca and the *alma* of Isaiah 7:14 and all other *almas* were virgin, until and unless it shall be proven that they were not. If Isaiah 7:14 is a prediction of the Conception and if the events recorded in Matthew 1:18-25 and Luke 1:26-38 are true and the Holy Spirit of God really overshadowed the Virgin Mary, all difficulties are cleared away. The language itself is not the difficulty.

The second argument against the Messianic application of this prophecy, is that the foretelling of the birth of a child centuries later would have conveyed no proof to Ahaz that the plottings of his enemies would be frustrated. On the surface the argument appears plausible. I fear that this has been the cause of stumbling to many Christians. Let us look into this prophecy a little more closely. There are two distinct declarations:

The first part of the prophecy assures the stability of the throne of the kingdom of Judah until the birth of the Son by the *h'alma* here foretold, and more distinctly spoken of again in *Isaiah chapter nine,* verses six and seven, and is in line with the prophecy made to Judah by his father Jacob, that "the sceptre shall not depart from Judah nor a lawgiver from between his feet, until Shiloh come" (Gen. 49:10). From the language employed in 7:13, "Hear ye now, O house of David: is it a small thing for you?" we see that the prophecy was not solely given to Ahaz, but to the "house of David," so that it included all the branches. This is clearly indicated by the use of plural pronouns "ye" and "you," which could not in the Hebrew be used in reference to a single person. The declaration while it gave assurance of safety for the time being to Ahaz, could not fail to give support and comfort at all times to his successors upon the throne of David.

The second part of the prophecy which was to assure Ahaz of a speedy deliverance from his invading enemies, is contained in *verse sixteen* of the seventh chapter. Ahaz, king of Judah, was under great anxiety lest his kingdom should be overthrown, and the house of David destroyed. Isaiah was sent and particularly directed to take his son Shear-jashub, who was then young, to assure the king that within sixty-five years the Syrian should be conquered, and Israel be carried away captive. The prophet was also to declare that before the child Shear-jashub should know how to refuse the evil and choose the good, that is, before the boy should arrive at years of discretion — that land should be forsaken of both her kings; as one rendering has it: "The land should become desolate, by whose kings he was distressed."

These two prophecies together assure Ahaz of deliverance from Syria and Israel. But in order to confirm their hopes, and at the same time make this temporal deliverance the means of leading their thoughts forward to still higher blessings, Isaiah, when Ahaz continued to refuse to ask that sign which God commanded him to ask, took occasion to give the most glorious and comforting sign, not to the house of David only, but to the whole human race, by predicting the birth of Messiah, who had been so long since foretold to come from that family. "The Lord Himself shall give you a sign; Behold, a *virgin* shall conceive, and bear a son, and shall call his name Immanuel." Both of these prophecies were fulfilled and we are the witness to God's faithfulness.

If there is one feature more conspicuous than another in the prophecies of Isaiah it is the prominence given to the thought of a Deliverer who should be raised up for the nation. The promises of God to Israel are rich in assurances of peace and abundance, of returning prosperity to Judah and a new glory to Zion; but they are to be fulfilled by the advent of One to whom should be the gathering of the peoples (Heb. *Amim,* Gen. 49:10; *Goim,* Isa. 11:10).. The one hope of the nation was in a man. He was to be of the root of Jesse, a son of David, endued with the Spirit of the Lord.

In Isaiah, chapter 9:1-6, we meet with the second *Immanuel* passage, although the name occurs twice in chapter 8:8 and 10, harking back to chapter 7:14-17, and shows that prophecy was not to be exhausted with Ahaz and his times. In the closing verse of chapter eight Isaiah pictures the desolation of Galilee by the Assyrian invasion, and "beholds trouble and darkness, dimness of anguish and utter gloom." But, here is the miracle of prophecy. Isaiah sees *Immanuel* coming first to Galilee, to a place that was held in low esteem in his day, just as it was in the days of Jesus. Here is God's message of hope through His faithful prophet:

> The people that walked in darkness have seen a great light: they that dwell in the land of the shadow of death, upon them hath the light shined. Thou hast multiplied the nation, not increased the joy: they joy before thee according to the joy in harvest, and as men rejoice when they divide the spoil. For thou hast broken the yoke of his burden, and the staff of his shoulder, the rod of his oppressor, as in the day of Midian. For every battle of the warrior is with confused noise, and garments rolled with blood; but this shall be with burning and fuel of fire. For unto us a child is born, unto us a son is given: and the government shall be upon his shoulder: and his name shall be called Wonderful, Counselor, The Mighty God, The everlasting Father, The Prince of Peace. Of the increase of his government and peace there shall be no end, upon the throne of David, and upon his kingdom, to order it, and to establish it with judgment and with justice from henceforth and even forever (Isa. 9:2-7).

In this we see Isaiah's positive conception of "Immanuel," the "Seed of the woman," the child of the virgin. The features of this conception are:

A. Immanuel's first ministry is to be in Galilee. In the New Testament record we find that *Matthew* in chapter 4: 13-16, speaks of the fulfillment of that "which was spoken by Esaias the prophet, saying: The land of Zabulon, and the land of Nephthalim, by the way of the sea, beyond Jordan, Galilee of the Gentiles" (vv. 14, 15). "On the ground of this prophecy of Isaiah," says Dr. Franz Delitzsch, "the Messianic hopes of the Jewish nation were really directed toward Galilee."[1]

B. The divine titles are *"Wonderful,"* the name by which God revealed Himself to Manoah and his wife as recorded in Judges 13:18: "Why askest thou after my name, seeing that it is secret?" (Hebrew *pele*), indicating thereby His divine nature: *"Counsellor"* corresponding with the Wisdom

[1] Dr. Delitzsch in his Commentary also says: "The Zohar was not the first to teach that the Messiah would appear in Galilee, and that redemption would break forth from Tiberias; but that this is found also in the Talmud and Midrash (see *Litteratur-blatt des Orients,* 1843, Col. 776).

of Proverbs; *"The Mighty God,"* El, the word for God, is linked to the name "Immanuel;" *"The Everlasting Father,"* is equivalent to the "Author of eternal salvation unto all that obey him" (Heb. 5:9); "The Prince of Peace," the name foreshadowed in the priestly King of Salem (Gen. 14:18), and in Solomon, the Peaceful One.

C. The characteristic features of the Davidic Covenant are also found here: He shall sit on David's throne; His kingdom is everlasting, and He is God's Son, as Jehovah had promised.

Iben Ezra, one of our honored Jewish commentators, says: "Some say that 'Wonderful, Counsellor, Mighty God, Everlasting Father' are the names of God (having in mind such commentators as Rashi, Kimchi, Abrabanel and the Malbim), but the right opinion in my mind is that all are the names of the Child."

But who is the Child?

The rabbis say that he is Hezekiah. This cannot be because Hezekiah was nine years old when his father Ahaz came to the throne, and our verses plainly describe the joy of the birth of one yet unborn when the prophet wrote. No, the Child cannot be Hezekiah. Nor is this Child Zerubbabel. For he did not accomplish much more than lead the first company of exiles home to Jerusalem, and play a rather unimportant part in the rebuilding of the Temple. There was nothing in his life that shall call forth an important prophecy as this is. Who then is He? Surely the Messiah, for it is He who is to be the Wonder-Counsellor, the Mighty God, the Everlasting Father, the Prince of Peace.

The third *Immanuel* passage is found in Isaiah 11:1-9 where we are introduced to several new features in Isaiah's picture of the Messiah. The tenth chapter, like the eighth, closes with a scene of desolation. Only the bare stumps remain to accentuate the desolation. Then comes this message of hope in the eleventh chapter. One of these stumps has life in it, and will put forth again, and it will be he who will usher in righteousness and peace to a world of strife. The sacred record states it:

> And there shall come forth a rod out of the stem of Jesse, and a branch shall grow out of his roots. And the spirit of the Lord shall rest upon him, the spirit of wisdom and understanding, the spirit of counsel and might, the spirit of knowledge and of the fear of the Lord. And he shall make him of quick understanding in the fear of the Lord; and he shall not judge after the sight of his eyes, neither reprove after the hearing of his ears; but with righteousness shall he judge the poor, and reprove with equity the meek of the earth; and he shall smite the earth with the rod of his mouth, and with the breath of his lips shall he slay the wicked. And righteousness shall be the girdle of his loins, and faithfulness the girdle of his reins. The wolf also shall dwell with the lamb, and the leopard shall lie down with the kid; and the calf and the young lion and the fatling together; and a little child shall lead them. And the cow and the bear shall feed; their young ones shall lie down together; and the lion shall eat straw like the ox. And the sucking child shall play on the hole of the asp, and the weaned child shall put his hand on the cockatrice' den. They shall not hurt nor destroy in all My holy mountain; for the earth shall be full of the knowledge of the Lord, as the waters cover the sea (Isa. 11:1-9).

This Messianic Age will not come as the result of some great popular revolution, the establishing of some New Deal or Fair Deal, but by the coming of a man who should be for an ensign of the people and the purpose of the divine mercy to be worked out. So was the hope which had dwelt for centuries in the heart of Israel, and which each prophet from Moses to Malachi had helped to foster and keep alive. To Isaiah it presented itself with special vividness. It was he who has given us that expressive figure, full at once of comfort and of strength — the man "who shall reign in righteousness . . . rule in judgment" and "shall be as an hiding-place from the wind and a covert from the tempest; as rivers of water in a dry place, as the shadow of a great rock in a weary land" (Isa. 32:2).

There is a grand impressiveness in the idea that through the ages God had been preparing the world for the coming of His Son, and that these prophets were heralds who were to tell of this heavenly Visitor, Immanuel.

In the following chapters and closing the first part of the book, Isaiah continues with his description of the Messianic Age. In chapter thirty-five, and under three figures we note —

1. *The transformed desert.* The wilderness through which redeemed Israel returns, is changed into a field of flowers.

> The wilderness and the solitary place shall be glad for them; and the desert shall rejoice, and blossom as the rose. It shall blossom abundantly, and rejoice; yea, with singing: the glory of Lebanon shall be given unto it, the splendor of Carmel and the plain of Sharon, they shall see the glory of the Lord and the excellency of our God (Isa. 35:1, 2).

2. *The healing of the human body, mind and spirit.*

> Strengthen ye the weak hands, and make the trembling knees strong. Say to them that are of a fearful heart, Be strong, fear not! Behold, your God will come for vengeance, for a divine retribution: He will come and bring you salvation. Then the eyes of the blind shall be opened, and the ears of the deaf shall be unstopped.. Then shall the lame man leap as an hart, and the tongue of the dumb sing:[2] for in the wilderness shall waters break out, and streams in the desert. And the parched ground shall become a pool, and the thirsty lands springs of water . . . (Isa.. 35:3-7).

3. *The redeemed flocking the highway on their way to Zion singing.*

> And an highway shall be there, and a way, and it shall be called The way of holiness (derech h'kodesh); the unclean shall not pass over it; but it shall be for those: the wayfaring man, even simple ones do not go astray. There will be no lion there, nor any ravenous beast shall go up thereon, shall not be found there; but the redeemed shall walk there: And the ransomed of the Lord shall return, and come to Zion with songs and everlasting joy upon their heads: they shall

---

[2] "The healing of bodily defects is merely the other side of what is actually effected by the coming of Jehovah" (Franz Delitzsch).

> obtain (lay hold of) joy and gladness, and sorrow and sighing shall flee away (Isa. 35:8-10).

The last section of the Book of Isaiah (ch. 38-66) embraces his ministry after the miraculous overthrow of Sennacherib's army. Chapters thirty-eight and thirty-nine are historical and introductory to what follows. The severe judgment that Judah had suffered and the miraculous deliverance that followed should have turned their hearts to the God of their fathers. But the hardness of heart foreshown in the vision of chapter six, with its fearful train of consequences, was not yet at an end. A better prince than Ahaz now sat on the throne. Hezekiah brought a new era of revival and prosperity for Judah; and to the public deliverance just experienced was added the individual mercy of a restoration from a mortal sickness. And yet, when the people were once again tried in their monarch, Hezekiah showed that he had not escaped the taint of the prevailing corruption. To the messengers of Merodach-baladan, king of Babylon, sent to congraulate him on his recovery, and perhaps also to induce him to join in a league against Assyria, Hezekiah who had on previous occasions displayed implicit trust in God, now exhibits all his treasuries. It was then that Isaiah appeared to announce to him the loss of his wealth, in which he prided himself and in which he placed a confidence that should have been placed in God alone. This exhibition which was designed to impress the king of Babylon with Hezekiah's greatness and power, served only to inflame cupidity:

> Behold, the days come, that all that is in thine house, and that which thy fathers have laid up in store until this day, shall be carried to Babylon; nothing shall be left, saith Jehovah. And of thy sons that shall issue from thee, which thou shalt beget, shall they take away; and they shall be eunuchs in the palace of the king of Babylon (Isa. 39:6, 7).

Those who refer the last part of Isaiah to an author or authors other than Isaiah, do so, in the main, from the fact that the standpoint taken is that of the captivity as actually existing,

and that consolation is offered the people in the promise of
deliverance. They claim that there is utter incongruity in
presenting consolation under a calamity which has not yet
occurred. "It is an absurdity," they say, "in threatening a
punishment for sin and in the next breath comforting those
who are to suffer it."

If this were a complete and fair statement from the historical point of view, we would be the last to criticize it. We
maintain that this representation of the case overlooks facts
and conditions which are vital in their importance, and are
quite sufficient to reverse our judgment.

What were the conditions which were potent enough
to call forth in the time of the prophet the *last twenty-seven
chapters* of the Book of Isaiah?

The prophet Isaiah had distinctly declared that conquest by
Babylon and captivity were surely to be visited upon the
nation. He did not allow the people to indulge in vain
exultation over the fall of Sennacherib, as though they were
henceforth safe from judgments. It was the prophet's mission
to point out the weightier woe before them, the last and the
sorest which he was commissioned to *foretell*. Yes, it was the
part of Isaiah to do for the days of trembling and discourage-
ment preceding the exile, what Ezekiel did during its actual
period. And their methods were not unlike. Both mingled
terrible warnings against the proud doers of iniquity with
comforting promises for the godly remnant. And both con-
cluded their missions with a glorious picture of Jehovah returning to dwell among his people and going forth from Zion
to bless and save mankind. Jehovah makes it a part of His
glory, according to Isaiah himself (42:8, 9) to declare new
things and tell his people of them "before they spring forth."
Of this glory modern critics would rob Him.

The comfort which Isaiah gives in chapters forty through
sixty-six, in the prospect of the Babylonian exile, is drawn,
as it has been stated by a great theologian, from "the mission

and destiny of the chosen people." It was not the purpose of God to cast away Judah as Israel had been cast away. The nation was not to perish, the blessing of Abraham was not to fail. The Messiah is not to be cut off from saving his people, and being a light to the Gentiles. What now shall bear up the hearts and the hopes of the godly among the people? What will keep their eyes fixed upon a more distant and glorious future? What will hold them in patriotic unity as a separate and distinct people? What will make them resolve to trust in Jehovah that they may yet be the vehicle of salvation to the whole world? What but a prophetic word as clear and as positive as that under which they had experienced judgment and affliction?

For the accomplishing of these great purposes, so vital in the history of Israel, no prophetic writing could be more wisely adapted than the Book of Isaiah from chapter forty to the close. *Chapters forty through forty-eight* contain a message of comfort and deliverance for Jehovah's people. *Chapters forty-nine through fifty-eight* describe Jehovah's Servant and His work. *Chapters fifty-eight through sixty-six* develop the future glories.

The first passage is found in chapter 41:8-20. The noticeable point in this section is:

The accumulation of titles in verse eight where we notice the following terms used to designate Jehovah's people: *Israel, Servant, Jacob, Chosen one, Abraham's seed.* This is no new idea but is taken directly from the covenant promise of the past (Ex. 19:5,6).

In the second passage, 42:1-7, we enter upon a new phase of the Servant development and the points to be noticed are the following:

A. Jehovah introduces His Servant, His Elect, called in righteousness (*tsedek*), who is especially prepared for the work of the gift of Jehovah's Spirit. The considerations which explain God's purpose in setting up a kingdom are the following:

1. Jehovah as the creator is the God of the nations.

2. Jehovah is not acknowledged by all the nations, but only by Israel, His chosen people.

3. By means of Israel Jehovah is to be universally known and acknowledged.

The Servant, Jehovah's righteousness, will deliver from sin and build His kingdom. But whom the Lord calls He will also qualify. He qualifies the Servant by putting the Spirit on Him. The endowment of the Spirit is to establish the righteousness and promote the glory of Jehovah, but especially and characteristically by a mission of mercy and comfort.

B. The methods of His work are unostentatious, inward, and spiritual (42:2). His methods are in striking contrast with —

1. The ritual display of idolatrous heathen.

2. The imperious manner of prophets like Elijah, or

3. The military display of such agents as Cyrus.

C. The work of the Servant is among the spiritually infirm (42:3,7). He deals with those who are blind and in prison and in spiritual bondage.

D. There is a double sphere for the Servant's ministry (42:1,4,6).

1. To Jehovah's people. To them He is a mediator of a New Covenant. The New Covenant is referred to no less than seven times in Isaiah. What covenant is this? It is not the covenant made with Noah (54:9,10), where this covenant is called the covenant of peace. It is not the old Sinaitic Covenant made through Moses, for that has been often broken by Israel. It is evidently the New Covenant described later in Jeremiah 31:31-34:

"Behold the days come, saith the Lord, that I will make a new covenant with the house of Israel, and with the house of Judah," etc., etc.

The covenant of Noah was a covenant of Providence with the race. The covenant with Abraham was a covenant of special Providence with a family. The covenant with Israel through Moses was a contract between Jehovah and a nation — a covenant of *love and defense* on one side, and of *obedience* on the other. The New Covenant is a covenant of mercy, of peace, and of spiritual fellowship with Jehovah. The Servant of Jehovah is the Mediator of this New Covenant as the main part of His work with the Chosen people.

2. To the nations: He is to establish judgment (*mishpat*) in the earth "unto truth" (*emeth*), and the isles shall wait for his law (Torah), revelation (Isa. 42:3, 4).

In chapter 43:1-7 there is a reaction in the prophet's mind to the first phase, that is, chapter forty-one. The prophet loved his people, and he clung for their sake to the promises for them made to Abraham and the fathers. How could he cast out his own Israel? But here we find that "Israel" is not national, but a redeemed Israel. Another instance of Isaiah's well-known doctrine of the saved remnant, with no reference to the mission of the Servant in a direct manner, is in preceding chapters. In chapters forty-two and forty-three the prophet is struggling with the fact of his people's sin. Here, redemption is the theme. Stern are the words with which the prophet denounces the old Israel after the flesh:

> But thou hast not called upon me, O Jacob; but thou hast been weary of me, O Israel. Thou hast not brought me the small cattle of thy burnt offerings; neither hast thou honored me with thy sacrifices. I have not made thee to serve with offerings, nor wearied thee with frankincense. Thou hast bought me no sweet cane with money, neither hast thou filled me with the fat of thy sacrifices: but thou hast made me to serve with thy sins, thou hast wearied me with thine iniquities. I, even I, am he that blotted out thy transgressions for my own sake: and I will not remember thy sins. Put me in remembrance; let us plead together: set thou forth thy cause, that thou mayest be justified (Isa. 43:22-26).

No student of the Bible can doubt that the Messianic idea is the haven of Old Testament prophecy. The Old Testament is the logbook which indicates the course of many tempestuous seas in Israel's history. George Adam Smith illustrates this truth thus: "The Messianic prophecies are tidal rivers. They not only run to their sea, which is Christ, they feel the reflex influence." The portion of the river nearest the sea shows most perceptibly the reflex influence, and in the streams of Messianic prophecy we are, in this latter part of the Book of Isaiah, nearest to the Christian age. We meet here for the first time with the anointed Leader, THE SERVANT OF JEHOVAH.

Who is this Servant of Jehovah? That was what the Ethiopian eunuch wanted to know. It is not difficult for us of this century to transport ourselves into the scene of the interview between this Ethiopian and the evangelist Philip. We have only to follow the most southern of the two roads which led from Jerusalem to Gaza which was the scene of the last great exploit of Samson, who terrorized the Philistines and avenged the people they molested for forty years. Close by there must have been the place where the eunuch's baptism had taken place. It should not surprise us that this stranger who had just been in Jerusalem to worship and where he was greatly impressed by both the Temple and the multitudes, should on this lonely road have busied himself with the Old Testament and in preference turned to its prophecies, and especially to that part of the Book of Isaiah where he met that mysterious Sufferer. He could not recognize His features. To this day Israel has failed to see in that face — more marred than any man's — the Messiah-King, the crown of its glory. How could that stranger know it? Hence his question: "I beg of you, about whom does the prophet say this? Of himself or of someone else?" (Berkeley Version).

We do not wonder then at his question. It is the same which in its ultimate idea, as the mystery of suffering, has engaged all thinking. It is that which has divided Jews from Christians through the centuries. How perplexing it has proved to the Synagogue appears not only from the widely divergent interpretations given by the rabbis, but even from their own admissions after these attempts have failed to solve its mystery.

THE NON-MESSIANIC INTERPRETATIONS

The most prevalent opinion among Jewish writers, present and past, is that by the Servant of Jehovah, whose suffering is here described, is meant *the nation of Israel*. According to them, Isaiah fifty-three describes the misery to which Israel is subjected, its steadfast adherence to the worship of the one living and true God amid the idolatry of the nations, and its final deliverance and glory. This opinion has been adopted and maintained by Iben Ezra, Rashi, David Kimchi, Lipmann, Adler and other Jewish writers. There are some among them, however, who restrict this prophecy to the pious portion of Israel. Thus Rashi, commenting on Isaiah 52:13: "Behold, my Servant shall be exalted and extolled, and be very high," explains the words: "Behold, in the latter days my servant Jacob shall prosper, that is, the righteous who are in his midst." Many of the Christian writers, who have adopted a non-Messianic interpretation, have also given a somewhat similar explanation but with a considerable diversity of opinion. "The theory," according to Dr. C. R. North, "has taken many forms, empirical Israel, ideal Israel, the pious remnant of the true Israel, the order of the prophets, together with combinations of these elements in different proportions."[3] Iben Ezra speaks of this prophecy as "extremely difficult," and Rabbi Moshe Kohen Iben Crispin of Toledo (14th century) says of those who for controversial reasons applied this prophecy to Israel that by so doing "the doors of the liberal interpretation of this Parashah were shut in their face, and that

[3] Christopher R. North, *The Suffering Servant*, p. 3.

they wearied themselves to find the entrance, having forsaken the knowledge of our teachers, and inclined after the stubbornness of their own hearts and of their own opinions."[4]

The second non-Messianic interpretation is, that by the Servant of Jehovah is meant the *prophetical order*. This opinion is not nearly so generally maintained as the idea that the nation of Israel is intended: Still it is adopted and defended by some theologians among whom are: Gesenius, DeWette, Umbreit and Hofmann. Umbreit remarks, "The Servant of Jehovah is the collective body of the prophets or the prophetical order, which is here represented as the sacrificial victim taking upon himself the sins of the people."[5]

The third non-Messianic view to be noted here is that by the Servant of Jehovah *an individual* is meant. The personal traits in this prophecy have led some to adopt this view. Bahardt fixed his eyes on Hezekiah, J. C. W. Augusti supposes that Uzziah is here meant, and Staudlin started from the rabbinical tradition that Isaiah was of royal birth, that he was martyred under Manasseh, and buried close by the kings, therefore applicable to the description of Isaiah fifty-three. The Abrabanel at first supposed that the nation of Israel was meant, but changed his opinion, and made King Josiah the subject of the prophecy. "The whole prophecy," he observes, "was uttered with reference to King Josiah." The person, however, who has been most frequently fixed upon is the prophet Jeremiah. This opinion was first introduced by Saadiah Gaon and afterwards repeated by others. Ewald was so struck with the personal characteristics of this prophecy that he dropped his former view that the ideal Israel is meant, and settled on some unknown sufferer — some single martyr.[6]

To such straits are the non-Messianic interpreters forced to

[4] David Baron, *Rays of Messiah's Glory.*
[5] Umbreit, *Den Knecht Gottes,* also North, *The Suffering Servant,* p. 38.
[6] Gloag's *Messianic Prophecies;* Edersheim; Oswald T. Allis, *The Unity of Isaiah.*

have recourse. Who then is this Servant of Jehovah? Is it the nation? Yes, sometimes; but not the present blind, disobedient, stiff-necked people Israel! Is this Servant of Jehovah an individual? Yes! Then who is he? Is he a Moses teaching a nation of pupils? Yes, and a greater than Moses; for the Servant has all nations for His pupils. Is he a Solomon? Yes, and a greater than Solomon is here, for the Servant has no national royalty. Is he one of the prophets, pleading intimately with Jehovah and prevailing? Yes, a greater than he; for this Servant is not struggling to prevail for Himself, but His victorious struggle and suffering avails for multitudes. He opened the kingdom of heaven to all believers of all nations, on the forgiveness, the peace, and the healing of body and soul, which He bought with His own blood. That was the fulfillment of Old Testament prophecy. And because He was the fulfillment of all, in type and promise, therefore was He the Messiah promised — the Hope of Israel and the Desire of all nations.

THE MESSIANIC INTERPRETATIONS

Mr. Ernest Gordon in an editorial in *The Sunday School Times* on "Who Was the Suffering Servant?" begins with the statement: "The early Jewish tradition regarding the fifty-third of Isaiah was Messianic. It was their controversy with Christianity which led the Jews to abandon this interpretation."[7] Mr. Gordon is right. Strange as it may seem to the modern Jew, our conclusion that "My Servant" meant Jesus of Nazareth, is borne out, supported and emphasized by the greatest writers of Talmudic and Medrashic literature. These ancient worthies conclude, without the shadow of a doubt, that the Messiah must suffer much for humanity's sake and that as a result of such suffering He shall be exalted and shall become the King of kings and Lord of lords.

We may now proceed to the exposition of Isaiah 52:13-

[7] *The Sunday School Times*, Aug. 25, 1951.

53:12 and notice the unfolding of this unique figure on the heart and mind of the prophet with some of the early rabbinical interpretations.

> Behold my servant shall deal wisely, he shall be exalted and lifted up, and shall be very high. Like as many were astonished at thee (his visage was so marred, more than any man, and his form more than the sons of man), so shall he sprinkle many nations; kings shall shout their mouths at him: for that which they had not been told them they shall see; and that which they had not heard shall they understand (Isa. 52: 13-15).

The Yalkut in its comments, says this passage refers to the Messiah because of the words "lifted up," "extolled" and "very high." He shall be higher than Abraham, to whom Genesis 14:22 applies; higher than Moses, Exodus 4:16; and greater than the angels, Ezekiel 1:18. But of the Messiah it is said, "Who art thou, O great mountain? Before Zerubbabel thou shalt become a plain and he shall bring forth the headstone thereof with shoutings, crying Grace, grace unto it"[8] (Zech. 4:7; see also Ps. 118:22; Phil. 2:9-11).

The Rambam in his letter to Timon says of the Messiah that "no one will know of his origin, but he will be recognized on account of the great miracles which he shall perform."

The earthly life of Israel's Messiah was full of woe and His end a tragedy; as a matter of fact those who were thus astonished at Him were wrong. The afflicted one arose from the dead, ascended to His Father in heaven, and when His followers began to preach and teach, kings and princes took notice of it and bowed their knees to Him.

Dr. Hengstenberg in his *Christology of the Old Testament* says, "The prophet in chapter 53 begins these presentations of the vicarious sufferings of the Messiah, he laments over the unbelief of a large portion of mankind. . . ."

The rabbis speak of a covenant God made with the Messiah at which time He said to Him, "Messiah My righteousness,

[8] *Yalkut*, a midrashic thesaurus on the whole of the Old Testament, 2-Par. 338.

the sins of those who are entrusted to Thee will impose a heavy yoke on Thee and make Thee like unto a calf whose eyes are heavy. On account of their sins Thy tongue will cleave to Thy palate for thirst, and Thy soul will be weakened by grief and sighing. Art Thou willing to undergo this?" The Messiah answered: "Lord of the universe, will this tribulation last many years?" God replied, "By Thy life, by Thy brow have I settled it by an oath. If Thy soul is oppressed with such a sorrow because of this, I will relieve Thee of it." Then said the Messiah: "Lord God of the universe, with joy and freedom of heart I take all this upon Me, that not one soul in Israel may be lost. This is My desire, and, with this understanding, I take upon Me all these sufferings, as it is written, 'He was oppressed, yet He humbled Himself.'"[9]

> Surely he hath borne our griefs, and carried our sorrows; yet we did esteem him stricken, smitten of God and afflicted. But he was wounded for our transgressions, he was bruised for our iniquities; the chastisement of our peace was upon him; and with his stripes we are healed. All we like sheep have gone astray; we have turned every one to his own way; and Jehovah hath laid on him the iniquity of us all (Isa. 53:4-6).

Rabbi Joshua ben Levi met Elijah whom he asked: "When will the Messiah come?" Elijah replied: "Go and ask Him, He sits at the gate among the sick and suffering. You will easily recognize Him. He binds up the wounds of every one separately."[10] This is in agreement with some of the other Jewish commentators. In the Messianic Age, our Fathers, Abraham, Isaac, Jacob and the prophets will say to the Messiah:

> Messiah, our Righteousness, although we are Thy forefathers, yet Thou art better than we, because Thou hast suffered for our sins and the sins of our children, and there have passed over Thee such as have not happened to the former generations or to those yet to come. Thou wast mocked and humiliated for Israel's sake, Thou didst dwell in darkness, Thy body

9 *Yalkut*, Amsterdam Edition, also P'siqta Rabbathi.
10 *Sanhedrin*, 97-99.

became lean and Thy eyes were darkened because of Thy fasting. All this happened on account of the sins of our children. Maybe on account of these sufferings art Thou unfriendly to them? Said He unto them: All that I have suffered I have done for your sake and for the sake of your children that you and they might be partakers of the goodness of God.[11]

He was oppressed, yet when he was afflicted he opened not his mouth; as a lamb that is led to the slaughter, and as a sheep that before its shearers is dumb, so he opened not his mouth. By oppression and judgment he was taken away; and as for his generation, who was among them considered that he was cut off out of the land of the living for the transgression of my people to whom the struck was due? And they made his grave with the wicked, and with the rich man in his death; although he had done no violence, neither was any deceit in his mouth (Isa. 53:7-9).

"He was oppressed, and He was afflicted, yet He opened not His mouth." Surely this cannot apply to the Jews. A glance at our own history will reveal that we have never behaved as little lambs in the face of danger and war. We never suffered evil without resistance.

George Adam Smith is right in observing:

Now silence under suffering is a strange thing in the Old Testament — a thing absolutely new. No other Old Testament personage could stay dumb under pain, but immediately broke into one of two voices — voice of guilt, or voice of doubt. In the Old Testament the sufferer is always either confessing his guilt to God, or, when he feels no guilt, challenging God in argument.[12]

Yet it pleased Jehovah to bruise him; he hath put him to grief: When thou shalt make his soul an offering for sin, he shall see his seed, he shall prolong his days, and the pleasure of Jehovah shall prosper in his hand. He shall see the travail of his soul, and shall be satisfied: by the knowledge of himself shall my righteous servant justify many; and he shall bear their iniquities. Therefore will I divide him a portion with the great, and he shall divide the spoil with the strong; because he poured out his soul unto death, and was numbered

[11] P'siqta Rabbathi, ed. Freedman. Also *Yalkut* on Isaiah.
[12] *The Book of Isaiah*, Vol. 2.

with the transgressors: yet he bare the sin of many, and made intercession for the transgressors (Isa. 53:10-12).

When the Holy One, blessed be His Name, shall make a feast for the righteous, the Messiah shall be among them. After the feast the Lord will honor Abraham, our father, with a cup of wine to make the blessing. Abraham will decline, saying, "I am unworthy because I have a son Ishmael." When Isaac will be requested, he will decline saying, "I had a son Esau." Jacob will decline and say, "I have two sisters for wives." When the turn comes to our great lawgiver, Moses, he too, will refuse, because he did not live to lead the children of Israel into the Promised Land and Joshua will refuse because he did not leave a son to take his place.

Then, when He shall come to David, he will accept the cup and say, "I am worthy to wind up the feast with a blessing, because the MESSIAH is descended from me. I will take up the cup of salvation (Joshua) and call upon the name of the Lord" (Ps. 116:13).

How shall we know HIM? Our God has made Him known unto our fathers and to us in unmistakable terms. "Sing, O heavens, and be joyful, O earth; and break forth into singing, O mountains; for the Lord hath comforted His people, and will have mercy upon His afflicted" (Isa. 49:13).

Our Musaph prayer for the Day of Atonement is noble in its longing and aspirations:

> Messiah, our righteousness, is departed from us; horror hath seized us, and we have none to justify us. He hath borne the yoke of our iniquities and our transgression, and is wounded because of our transgressions. He beareth our sins on His shoulder, that He may find pardon for our iniquities. We shall be healed by His wounds. O Eternal One, it is time that Thou shouldest create Him anew. O bring Him up from the circle of the earth, rise Him up from Seir, to assemble us the second time on Mount Lebanon, by the hand of *Yinnon*.[13]

13 "Yinnon" is a Talmudic term for the Messiah (*Sanhedrin*, 98b).

CHAPTER VI

MESSIANIC PROPHECY DURING THE ASSYRIAN AND BABYLONIAN INVASIONS
(Nahum, Habakkuk, Zephaniah, Jeremiah)

NAHUM

"God is jealous, and Jehovah revengeth; Jehovah revengeth and is full of wrath; Jehovah will take vengeance on His adversaries, and He reserveth wrath for His enemies" (Nah. 1:2). This is the theme of the prophecy of Nahum, the approaching capture and sack of the cruel capital of the Assyrian empire, "The burden of Nineveh." The use of the Hebrew word *massa* as well as *chazon* denotes a divine revelation and the claim to inspiration. And although its message is entirely to the downfall of the Assyrian power and the destruction of its capital city, not threatening directly either Judah or Israel, nevertheless, the book is highly significant in its character and teachings. Its teachings touch some of the central truths of the Scriptures and are in profound and happy accord with doctrines set forth in both the Old and the New Testaments.

The sublime and spiritual understanding of God's character (1:1,2), is the basis on which the prophet rests the threatenings and the promises of the book. The side of retributive righteousness is turned toward the cruel oppressor. "Jehovah is good, a stronghold in the day of trouble; and He knoweth them that take refuge in Him" (1:7). All the rest of the prophecy is the application in a particular case of the general principles there laid down in depth and accuracy of spiritual

93

insight by Nahum, the compassionate, a name that refers back to Jehovah's compassion connected with Jonah's mission to Nineveh years before. Nothing is known of Nahum beyond this book, which sets before us his name and the place of his birth (1:1). The time of the writing of this prophecy can be determined only from the allusions in the book itself and in the light of sacred and secular history. This should lead us to place him somewhere between 661 B.C. and 612 B.C.[1]

The prophecy, when taken in connection with the Book of Jonah, reveals some valuable spiritual lessons. In Jonah we learn that God is no respecter of persons, but that in every nation, he that worketh righteousness is acceptable to Him. In Nahum we see penitent Nineveh having received the salvation which, by the grace of God, was offered to them, now turn to despise the goodness of God, and in deceit and cruelty, in persistent wickedness move on to her doom. What do we find then? We find that the same God, because He is ever the same, who forgave before, will now destroy; and we learn now not less than in the Book of Revelation, to dread "the wrath of the Lamb" (Rev. 6:16).

There seems to be little of Messianic prophecy in the Book of Nahum, and many writers on the subject seem to pass it over. Professor Klausner explains this scarcity:

> not alone by the fact that only three chapters of this prophet have reached us. I have already pointed out once that I do not believe that many important Messianic prophecies were lost or forgotten in the course of time. The Hebrew people guarded Messianic prophecies of this kind as the apple of its eye. Thus it is impossible that the Messianic prophecies of Nahum are few because some of them were lost.[2]

The cause of this scarcity lies within the book itself. Nahum's main message was concerning the fall of Nineveh, and the end which would soon come to the kingdom of Assyria. When

---

[1] Kleinert Strauss, Franz Delitzsch, Kirkpatrick and Klausner.
[2] *The Messianic Idea in Israel,* pp. 79, 80.

that happens, that is, the destruction of those who have
troubled God's chosen people, Nahum calls upon them to —
> Behold upon the mountains the feet of Him that bringeth
> good tidings, that publisheth peace! Keep thy feasts, O Judah,
> perform thy vows: for the wicked shall not pass through; he
> is utterly cut off (Nah. 1:15; Heb. 2:11).[3]

HABAKKUK

We know little about the prophet Habakkuk apart from
his book, and even here we are not told all we would like to
know about him. There are some who hold that the prophet
was speaking against the Greeks, while others date the
prophecy to the reign of Jehoiakim (609 to 598 B.C.), which
would also be the years in which Nebuchadnezzar besieged
Jerusalem and carried away Daniel among the captives. He
follows closely the time of Nahum, whose prophecy as we
have seen deals with Assyria; this one deals with the Chaldeans. However, from his message, it would seem that he
prophesied as early as the reign of Manasseh (687-642 B.C.),
who foolishly played politics with the Babylonian envoys
(II Kings 20:12-19) and thereby brought forth Israel's prophecy of the forthcoming Chaldean invasion. There is good
reason for the remarks the prophet makes concerning them.
Micah and Isaiah had already predicted the downfall of
Judah at the hands of the Chaldeans. That had not happened
as yet, so it would seem from the statements of 2:20 and
3:19b. All this seems to lead some students to place Habakkuk's ministry during the days of Manasseh (II Kings 21:
10-15).

The three short chapters which deal with the last of these
three world powers, Babylon, contain messages of lasting
worth. The book begins with a complaint to God, and that
is the real burden:
> O Lord, how long shall I cry, and thou wilt not hear? I
> cry unto thee of violence, and thou wilt not save. Why dost
> thou show me iniquity, and cause me to look upon perverseness?

[3] Cf. Isaiah 52:7.

> For destruction and violence are before me; and there is strife, and contention riseth up. Therefore the law [Torah] is slacked, and justice doth never go forth; for the wicked doth compass about the righteous; therefore justice goeth forth perverted (1: 1-4).

There is much more of complaining. Look at the invaders:

> They come all of them for violence; the set of their faces is towards the east; and they gather captives as the sand. Yea, they scoff at kings and princes are a derision unto them; they laugh at every fortress, they heap up earth and take it. Then shall he sweep by as a wind, and shall pass over and be guilty; imputing this his power unto his god (1:9-11).

"How long, O Lord, how long?" The prophet believes God and therefore will not despair. God does not fail him. Here is the answer:

> And Jehovah answered me and said, Write the vision, and make it plain upon the tablets, that he may run who reads it. For the vision is yet for the appointed time, and it hasteth toward the end, and shall not lie: though it tarry, wait for it; because it will surely come, it will not delay. Behold, his soul is puffed up, it is not upright in him; but the righteous shall live by his faith (2:2-4).

Then the prophet reaches out into the heights of God's great plan of salvation and the ultimate victory for His people:

> For though the fig-tree shall not flourish,
> Neither shall fruit be in the vines;
> The labor of the olive shall fail,
> And the fields shall yield no food;
> The flocks shall be cut off from the fold,
> And there shall be no herd in the stalls:
> Yet I will rejoice in Jehovah,
> I will joy in the God of my salvation.
> Jehovah, the Lord, is my strength;
> And He maketh my feet like hind's feet,
> And will make me to walk upon my high places. (3:17-19.)

This coming deliverance is the same deliverance which is ever looked for in the unfolding of the divine side of Messianic prediction. It is said that Daniel Webster considered Habakkuk, chapter 3:17-19, as the most beautiful passage in the Bible. In a time of poverty and famine; no flocks, no herds, no crops; "Yet I will rejoice in the Lord, I will joy in the God of my salvation." Paul's admonition to those who came to God through Christ Jesus our promised Messiah, has been in the same line: "Rejoice in the Lord alway: and again I say, rejoice" (Phil. 4:4).

ZEPHANIAH

Zephaniah, whose name means "hidden of God," was probably of princely birth. He has recorded no details about himself except his lineage which is traced back four generations to Hezekiah, king of Judah. He does not say Hezekiah, king of Judah, but it has been assumed by most commentators including Iben Ezra, that Zephaniah is descended from King Hezekiah, who reigned during the days of Isaiah. He prophesied during the reign of Josiah, king of Judah (640-608 B.C.), and may have helped forward the reforms inaugurated by the young king.

Zephaniah is known chiefly for his description of the day of Jehovah's wrath against sinners. Under the shadow of that day of darkness the prophet cries:

> Hold thy peace at the presence of the Lord God: for the day of the Lord is at hand: for the Lord hath prepared a sacrifice, he hath bid his guests. . . . The great day of the Lord is near, it is near, and hasteth greatly, even the voice of the day of the Lord: the mighty men shall cry there bitterly. The day is a day of wrath, a day of trouble and distress, a day of wasteness and desolation, a day of darkness and gloominess, a day of clouds and thick darkness. A day of the trumpet and alarm against the fenced cities, and against the high towers. And I will bring distress upon men, that shall walk like blind men, because they have sinned against the Lord: and their blood shall be poured out as dust, and their flesh as the dung. Neither their silver nor their gold shall be able to deliver them in the day of the Lord's wrath; but the whole land shall be devoured by the fire of his jealousy: for he shall make even a speedy riddance of all them that dwell in the land (1:7, 14-18).

Heavy judgment will overtake the Gentiles. Zephaniah describes the destruction of the cities of the Philistines. Moab and Ammon will become like Sodom and Gomorrah, the Ethiopians will be slain by the sword and Assyria and Nineveh will cease to exist. This is universal judgment for the purpose of redemption, a redemption not only for Israel but also for the nations; hence his appeal to all:

> Seek ye the Lord, all ye meek of the earth, which have wrought his judgment: seek righteousness, seek meekness: it may be ye shall be hid in the day of the Lord's anger (2:3).

The prophecy is naturally divided into three parts. The first is the announcement of the rapidly approaching day of the judgment upon the nations, especially upon Judah, chapter one. The second consists of an appeal based upon the foregone decree of judgment and the further prophecy that the heathen powers of the four quarters of the earth shall be overthrown, chapter 2:1 to 3:7. The third part completes the book, 3:8-20, and consists of a glorious promise of restoration and salvation to the remnant of Israel who are true to Jehovah.

Judgment complete and final is the message of God through Zephaniah. Amid the dense darkness there appears the glorious purpose of the Most High to redeem unto Himself a holy people and thereby vindicate His administration of the world, and magnify His Name. The Messianic chain, sin, punishment, repentance, redemption, is discernible in the Messianic prophecies of Zephaniah.[4] He begins with woe, and ends with singing:

> Sing, O daughter of Zion; shout O Israel; be glad and rejoice with all thy heart, O daughter of Jerusalem. The Lord hath taken away thy judgments, he hath cast out thine enemy: The King of Israel, even the Lord is in the midst of thee: thou shalt not see evil any more (3:14, 15).

[4] *The Messianic Idea in Israel*, p. 82.

Jeremiah

Three of the four Major Prophets of the Old Testament belong to the historical period of the Babylonian exile and its immediately anterior years. The prophets Jeremiah, Ezekiel and Daniel found themselves so involved in the national and moral problems of their time that they were led to say little concerning the future. Nevertheless there are some exceedingly interesting Messianic messages in these books. A few chapters in the heart of the Book of Jeremiah and near the end of Ezekiel, and the second part of the Book of Daniel, offer more fertile fields for Messianic expression than other parts of these books.

The century that intervened between the last Messianic utterances of the prophet Isaiah and the time of Jeremiah was full of stirring events in the political world of that time. The Assyrian lion who had long terrified the inhabitants of that part of Asia was beginning to decline. Esarhaddon (II Kings 19:37; Isa. 37:38) undertook the conquest of Egypt, and Ashurbanipal achieved it. "The one pierced far into the mountains," says one historian, "while the latter subjugated Elam." Throughout the years of these kings, Judah remained for the most part in a state of vassalage to Assyria. Within Judah a lamentable reaction had followed the death of Hezekiah. During the reign of Manasseh there was a wave of persecution and tradition says that the old prophet himself was a victim of his wrath. It was not until the accession of Josiah that the violence of the persecution stopped. After the death of Ashurbanipal, Assyria went rapidly to its fall, and Babylon, for a long time a dependent province, fell away, and united with the newly appearing nation of Media. Meanwhile, the Scythians poured through the passes of the Caucasus, covered the rich plains of the south and spread destruction over the entire field of western Asia. Judah was then involved in the battle which arose in connection with the fall of Nineveh. Necho, the king of Egypt (II Kings 23:29), who came up to restrain the Asiatic predominancy, was defeated in the battle of Carchemish and this brought about the coming of Babylon as the mistress of the anterior of Asia, the passing of Judah into the hands of Nebuchadnezzar who in time caused Judah's downfall and destruction.

Against this dark picture of threat and punishment, there appeared glorious Messianic promises. Like Isaiah, a century before, Jeremiah, whose message is that of judgment against Judah and a call to "Amend your ways and your doings, and I will cause you to dwell in this place" (7:3), is permitted to see Him "of whom Moses in the law, and the prophets did write" (John 1:45):

> Behold, the days come, saith the Lord, that I will raise unto David a righteous Branch, and a King shall reign and prosper, and shall execute judgment and justice in the earth. In his days Judah shall be saved, and Israel shall dwell safely: and this is his name whereby he shall be called, THE LORD OUR RIGHTEOUSNESS [Jehovah-tsidkenu]. Therefore behold, the days come, saith the Lord, that they shall say no more, the Lord liveth, which brought up the children of Israel out of the land of Egypt: but, the Lord liveth, which brought up and led the seed of the house of Israel out of the north country, and from all countries whither I had driven them; and they shall dwell in their own land (Jer. 23:5-8).

We have here the first Messianic prophecy. It began with the description of the wicked shepherds, who misled and despoiled the flock of Jehovah and quickly turns from the equally unworthy kings to the ideal King of the Messianic Hope, whose name is — JEHOVAH OUR RIGHTEOUS-NESS." Says Dr. Franz Delitzsch,

> Many interpreters draw the conclusion, because the promise concerning the awakening of right shepherds (23:4) precedes, that the sprout is intended collectively [as] an aftergrowth of Davidic rulers who are pleasing God; but [from] the repeated prophecy of the "Branch" in 33:14-16 this view is without support, the promise is with reference to one, and the progress from the *branch* of Isaiah 4:2 to the shoot from the stump of Jesse of Isaiah 11:1 makes it unquestionable that the prophet means

that the Messiah is the second David (*Messianic Prophecies*, p. 182).

The chief Messianic section in Jeremiah is found in chapters thirty through thirty-three and is one of the noblest passages of the Old Testament. "The strain of confident hope in the future," says one commentator, "is sustained throughout the whole passage. Without these chapters the great prophet might be considered a John the Baptist of denunciation or a prophet of pessimism." Here the prophet turns aside from things present, distasteful and heart-sickening, to the future. In a vision he sees the exiles on their homeward journey — a great company returning to Zion, among them the blind and the lame and the women with child, no one left behind, weeping as they go for their former sins, yet in God's mercy finding their way to the place of rest (Jer. 31:1-9). Next we witness a harvest-home feast celebrated by returned exiles, when the voice of song is heard, and the virgin rejoices in the dance, and all, young and old, forget their sorrow because of the goodness of the Lord in filling their barns and causing their flock to multiply (Jer. 31:10-14). Then we hear the lamentations of a woman weeping bitterly. It is Mother Rachel weeping for her dead children, and God saying to her, "Refrain thy voice from weeping and thine eyes from tears for thy work shall be rewarded, saith the Lord, and they shall come again from the land of the enemy" (Jer. 31:15, 16). Last comes the most pathetic scene of all. What we see now is not Rachel weeping for her children, but the children weeping for themselves — Ephraim repenting and full of grief over his youthful folly, confessing his sins and admitting that the severe treatment he had received had been fully deserved; and, at some distance from the penitent, God overhearing the contrite words of the prodigal child is saying:

> I have surely heard Ephraim bemoaning himself thus; Thou hast chastened me, and I was chastised, as a bullock unaccustomed to the yoke: turn thou me and I shall be turned; for

thou art the Lord my God. Surely after that I was turned, I
repented; and after that I was instructed, I smote upon my
thigh: I was ashamed, yea, even confounded, because I did
bear the reproach of my youth. Is Ephraim my dear son? Is
he a pleasant child? for since I spake against him, I do earnestly
remember him still: therefore my bowels are troubled for him:
I will surely have mercy upon him, saith the Lord (Jer. 31:
18-20).

What a vision of Israel's future! "Upon this I awaked,"
says Jeremiah, "and beheld; and my sleep was sweet unto me"
(Jer. 31:26). But the joy of the prophet might be checked
by the intrusion of a doubt as to the stability of that happy
future which had been revealed to him in vision. He could
hardly help asking himself the question: What is the use
of restoring Israel, if the old tragic disappointing history is
to repeat itself? Had not God shown measureless patience to
this people He had chosen and they failed Him again and
again? What if all this should happen over again in the
history of our children as it happened in the days of our
fathers? How natural and how human these fears are! They
constituted, we may be sure, one of his direst spiritual trials.
But faith's trials, are but the precursors of new triumphs:

> Behold, the days come, saith the Lord, that I will make
> a new covenant with the house of Israel, and with the house
> of Judah: Not according to the covenant that I made with
> their fathers in the day that I took them by the hand to bring
> them out of the land of Egypt; which my covenant they brake,
> although I was an husband unto them, saith the Lord: But
> this shall be the covenant that I will make with the house
> of Israel; after those days, saith the Lord, *I will put my law
> in their inward parts,* and write it in their hearts; and will
> be their God, and they shall be my people. And they shall
> teach no more every man his neighbor, and every man his
> brother, saying, Know the Lord: for they shall all know me,
> from the least of them unto the greatest of them saith the
> Lord: for I will forgive their iniquity, and I will remember
> their sin no more (Jer. 31:31-34).

An examination of this prophecy reveals some outstanding
peculiarities of the New Covenant:

1. That the prophet's hope of the permanent well-being of the people in the future will not be based on any expectation of the people doing better, but rather on the faith that God in His grace will do more for them and in them. He is the Doer, man is the subject of His gracious action. He is the Giver, man is the receiver. It was said of old, "If ye will obey my voice in deed, and keep my covenant, then ye shall be a peculiar treasure unto me above all people; for all the earth is mine. And ye shall be unto me a kingdom of priests, and an holy nation" (Ex. 19:5,6). There is no "if," suspending God's blessing and favor on man's good behavior. God promises absolutely to be their God, and to regard them as His people forever.

2. The New Covenant to be introduced is on the express ground of the dissatisfaction and failure of the old. In the case of the old the law of duty was written on *tables of stone;* in the case of the new, the law is to be written on the *heart*. In the case of the old, owing to the ritual character of worship, the knowledge of God and His will was a complicated affair in which one was generally helplessly dependent on a professional class. Under the new, the worship of God would be reduced to the simplest spiritual elements, and it would be in every man's power to know God at first hand. Finally, there is the old question, the provisions for the cancelling of sin which were unsatisfactory, and utterly unfit to perfect the worshiper as to his conscience, by dealing thoroughly with the problem of guilt. Under the new, on the contrary, God would grant to His people a real, absolute, and perennial forgiveness so that the abiding relation between Him and them should be as if sin had never existed. "I will put the law in their inward parts, and write it in their hearts." Writing on the heart is more intimate, more durable than in the ark. And that is what Jeremiah puts in the forefront in his account of the New Covenant, on which restored Israel is to be constituted and of

which Peter speaks in one of his sermons (Acts 3:21) as "the times of restoration of all things."

Jeremiah sees the line of David hastening to a physical end. Four kings in succession, Jehoahaz, Jehoiakim, Jehoiachin and Zedekiah have proved unfaithful and unfit. But a covenant was made with Abraham, Jacob and David, which cannot be annulled. Therefore a greater Son David with an endless reign in justice and righteousness must arise in the future. Hence, the added promise:

"Thus saith the Lord; if ye can break my covenant of the day, and my covenant of the night, and there should not be day and night in their season; then may also my covenant be broken with David my servant, that he should not have a son reign upon his throne" (Jer. 33:20, 21).

This is certainly in line with Isaiah's vision of the future kingdom (Isa. ch. 4 and 11), with Micah's return to Bethlehem for a king (Mic. ch. 4 and 5), and with the original Davidic covenant with David (II Sam. 7 and Ps. 89).

Jeremiah is the prophet who combines the glorious future for Israel and the world with the renewal of the covenant and he uses the word BRITH CHADASHA, the New Covenant — the name of the New Testament which with the Old Testament completes God's revelation to mankind.

CHAPTER VII

MESSIANIC PROPHECY DURING AND AFTER THE BABYLONIAN EXILE
(Ezekiel, Daniel, Haggai, Zechariah, Malachi)

EZEKIEL

The reader will recall that Ezekiel, a true prophet of God, began his ministry "among the captives by the river of Chebar" (1:1), declaring the wickedness of his people, calling them "impudent children"; "impudent and stiff-hearted" and "a rebellious nation" (2:3,4). God speaking through him, says,

> Behold, I, even I, am against thee; and I will execute judgment in the midst of thee in the sight of the nations. And I will do in thee that which I have not done . . . I will make thee a desolation and a reproach among the nations that are round about thee. . . . Destruction cometh; and they shall seek peace, and there shall be none (5:8,9,14; 7:25).

After thus addressing the people, and the land, and all those who comforted themselves in the thought that the city was impregnable (ch. 1-24), the prophet speaks to the surrounding nations (ch. 25-32 and 35) and then turns again to Israel, this time with a cluster of precious promises. The nations insulted Israel as a land whose ancient high places were their prey, a land that devoured its inhabitants. God takes occasion from this to show that He favors His people and declares that He will restore peace and prosperity to the land and take away their reproach.

> Therefore say unto the house of Israel, Thus saith the Lord Jehovah: I do not do this for your sake, O house of Israel, but for my holy name, which ye have profaned among the

nations, whither ye went. And I will sanctify my great name, which hath been profaned among the nations, which ye have profaned in the midst of them; and the nations shall know that I am Jehovah, saith the Lord Jehovah, when I shall be sanctified in you before their eyes. For I will take you from among the nations, and gather you out of all the countries, and will bring you into your own land. And I will sprinkle clean water upon you, and ye shall be clean from all your filthiness, and from all your idols, will I cleanse you. A new heart will I give you, and a new spirit will I put within you; and I will take away the stony heart out of your flesh, and I will give you a heart of flesh. And I will put my Spirit within you, and cause you to walk in my statutes, and ye shall keep my ordinances, and do them. And ye shall dwell in the land that I gave to your fathers; and ye shall be my people, and I will be your God (Ezek. 36:22-28).

Here are the revealed purposes of God concerning His people Israel. This is indeed the only note of encouragement which the prophet could give, for how can there be fulfillment of any of the promises of the past unless Israel is restored to her native land:

A. *Israel's Restoration.* "I will take you from among the nations, and gather you out of all the countries." The Egyptian redemption is only a faint picture, a type of what is yet to happen to Israel. Isaiah's cheering note makes the picture brighter as he tells of the nations who will help them in their return. "And they shall bring all your brethren as an offering unto Jehovah, out of all nations upon horses, and in chariots and covered cars, upon mules, and upon dromedaries, to My holy mountain, to Jerusalem" (Isa. 66:20).

B. *Israel's Purgation.* "I will sprinkle clean water upon you, and ye shall be clean." The prophet-priest was well acquainted with the sacrificial rites and probably refers to Numbers twenty. As the individual Jew was purged from his defilement by this sacrificial sprinkling, so will the Jews as a nation find cleansing by the cleansing power of the Lord Jesus, whose pierced side forms the fountain opened to the house of David and the inhabitants of Jerusalem for sin and uncleanness (Zech. 13:1).

C. *Israel's Regeneration.* "A new heart will I give you." Repentant Israel will at last find forgiveness, not through the castigation of thirty-nine strokes with a strap on the bare back administered by the Shammash (Sexton) of the Synagogue, or through fasting and the giving of charity, but through God's gift of a new heart. Israel will experience a new birth. A new nation will come into being, with new thoughts, new emotions and new affections. With the new heart and renewed spirit everything will be changed, prejudices and hatred will give way to love and adoration. Reborn Israel will welcome the long-hoped-for promised Messiah, crying, "Blessed is He that cometh in the name of the Lord" (Isa. 25:9; Ps. 118:26; Matt. 22:39).

D. *Israel's Sanctification.* "I will cause them to walk in My statutes." The Hebrew word *veasith* carries the thought that God will make it that they shall walk in His statutes, a new spiritual force will be imparted to them that will delight to do His will. The promise, "ye shall be my people," recalls the promise and assurance given back in Egypt, "I will take you to Me for a people and I will be your God" (Ex. 6:7), and through Jeremiah (32:40) and in Ezekiel (37:26).

> I will make an everlasting covenant with thee, and I will not turn away from them to do them good; but I will put my fear in their heart and they shall not depart from me. . . . Moreover I will make a covenant of peace with them: and it shall be an everlasting covenant . . . yea, I will be their God and they shall be my people.

The thirty-seventh chapter of Ezekiel carries the same message of hope and victory. The prophet was set down in the valley full of bones, and they were dry: and he prophesied upon them, according to the commandment of God, and they lived, and stood up, an exceeding great army, (vv. 1-10). What was the meaning of this vision? The author of the vision shall himself explain:

> Then he said unto me, Son of man, these bones are the whole house of Israel; behold, they say, Our bones are dried up, and our hope is lost; we are clean cut off. Therefore prophesy, and say unto them, Thus saith the Lord Jehovah: Behold, I will open your graves, and cause you to come out of your graves, O my people; and I will bring you into the land of Israel. And ye shall know that I am Jehovah, when I have opened your graves, and caused you to come up out of your graves, O my people. And I will put my Spirit into you, and ye shall live, and I will place you in your own land: then shall ye know that I, Jehovah, have spoken it and performed it, saith Jehovah (Ezek. 37:11-14).

In the latter part of the thirty-seventh chapter there is the record of an emblematic transaction, showing the union of the two branches of the nation after their return, and looking forward to the better days of the Messiah, when all things foreshadowed would be fully enjoyed. The prophet, by divine direction, took two sticks, and wrote upon them for the two branches of the nation, and joined them in his hand as one stick, signifying that the two branches of the nation should again become united in one.

"I will make them one nation in the land upon the mountains of Israel; and one king shall be king over them all — David my servant shall be king over them; and they shall have one shepherd" (vv. 22, 24).

This act of joining the two sticks sets forth in unmistakable terms Israel's national reunion which is to take place when Israel is restored and regathered from among the nations where they have been scattered and brought back to their own land. This reunion is to be accomplished during the reign of the Messiah, their Shepherd King.

This restoration is to be followed by an invasion of their land and is recorded in the well-known Gog and Magog chapters thirty-eight and thirty-nine; but the armies of these uncircumcised will find a place of graves, and the debris of the battlefield will supply Israel with firewood. Ezekiel's Armageddon is the climax of an age-long conflict, involving all nations, with the final stage to be fought and won in the land of Israel.

In Ezekiel forty through forty-eight, there is a vision of a city, and a temple, larger than the earliest ones. It is to be for worshipers of all nations.

> And it shall come to pass in the latter days that the mountain of Jehovah's house shall be established on the top of the mountains, and shall be exalted above the hills; and all nations shall flow unto it. And many peoples shall go and say, Come ye, and let us go up to the mountain of Jehovah, to the house of the God of Jacob; and he will teach us of his ways, and we will walk in his paths: for out of Zion shall go forth the law, and the word of Jehovah from Jerusalem (Isa. 2:2, 3).

The same vision was seen by Zechariah; "All that are left of all the nations that came against Jerusalem shall even go up from year to year to worship the King, Jehovah of Hosts, and to keep the feast of Tabernacles" (Zech. 14:16). It will be "a house of prayer for all nations." What a glorious picture! Israel's enemies having been crushed, the glory returns, the temple is built, Jesus is worshiped as King over all the earth, and the Holy City shall be named *Jehovah Shammah*, the Lord is there. So Ezekiel keeps in line with all the prophets in proclaiming "the sure mercies of David," the inviolability of the Messianic covenant, which Jehovah made with David.

Truly, "Eye hath not seen, nor ear heard, neither have entered into the heart of man, the things which God hath prepared for them that love Him. But God hath revealed them unto us by His Spirit: for the Spirit searcheth all things, yea, the deep things of God" (I Cor. 2:9, 10).

It has been said by some commentators that "Ezekiel was the prolongation of the voice of Jeremiah." "This," they say, "is certainly evident in the life and writings of Ezekiel."[1]

This should not be considered a total dependence on the part of Ezekiel. What he wished to do was to point out the

[1] G. Campbell Morgan, *The Message of Ezekiel.*

"common foundation of his agency, and of the older servant of God, to the essential unity of God's Word, notwithstanding the individual diversity of the human instrument who uttered it."[2]

Jeremiah announced the Babylonian exile, but Ezekiel lived in it. When King Jehoiachin had been dethroned by Nebuchadnezzar in 597 B.C., Ezekiel was among the nobles, warriors and priests who were then carried into Babylon (II Kings 23:14-16). He was the spiritual leader of the congregation in their captivity, which he often called "our captivity." His commission said: "Go, get thee to them of the captivity, unto the children of thy people, and speak unto them, and tell them, thus saith the Lord God; whether they will hear, or whether they will forbear" (Ezek. 3:11).

Ezekiel's mission was to teach the Jews of the captivity Jehovah's plan for the restoration of His people. Their hopes were set upon a speedy return from the exile and upon the rehabilitation of Jerusalem and Judea. It was Ezekiel's commission to shatter these hopes, and to convince them that Jehovah had left His city and given it over to their enemies as a punishment for its sins. Jerusalem stained with the blood of God's prophets, Jerusalem defiled beyond description by her unfaithfulness to Jehovah must be overthrown. A complete breaking with the past was the indispensable condition of restoration to divine favor.

This book may be divided into three parts:

Part 1, chapters one through twenty-four. The testimonies from God against Israel in general and against Jerusalem in particular. In chapter seven the prophet announces the catastrophic end in terse language:

> An end cometh, the end is come: it watches for thee, behold, it is come. The calamitous end is come against thee, O thou that dwellest in the land: the time is come, the day of trouble is near, a tumultuous noise and not the joyous shout of the mountains (vv. 6, 7).

[2] Hengstenberg, *Christology*, iii, p. 458.

In verse twenty-four the Babylonians are called "the evil of the nations." These were to come and take possession of the homes of the people, cause their pride to cease, defile their holy places and cause destruction everywhere: "Calamity upon calamity cometh, and evil report after evil report.... The king shall mourn, the prince shall be clothed with desolation, and the hands of the people of the land shall be troubled: I will do unto them after their way, and according to their deserts will I judge them; and they shall know that I am the Lord" (Ezek. 7:26, 27).

Israel is often portrayed in the Bible under the figure of a vine or a vineyard (Isa. 5; Ps. 80:8). Jehovah speaks of this to Ezekiel:

> Son of man, what is the vine tree more than any tree, or than a branch which is among the trees among the forest? . . . Behold, it is cast into the fire for fuel; the fire devoureth both the ends of it, and the midst of it is burned. Is it meet for any work? Ezek. 15:2, 4).

In Isaiah 5:4 the complaint is:

"What could have been done more to my vineyard that I have not done to it? Wherefore, when I looked that it should bring forth grapes, brought it forth bad grapes?"

Thus Ezekiel's message is in harmony with God's messages concerning Israel. The last of these prophecies was delivered two years before the fall of the city. Between these dates, 588 B.C., and the arrival of tidings of Jerusalem's destruction, falls the second section.

Part II, chapters twenty-five through thirty-two — judgments denounced against the nations. While waiting for the tidings which would confirm his prophecy of doom for the city, whose cup of iniquity was full, the prophet took up the accountability of the nations at the judgment bar of Jehovah just as Jeremiah did at the end of his book. Why such threatenings? Because the neighbors of Israel "had clapped the hands, and stamped with the feet, and rejoiced in heart," at Jerusalem's fall (25:6) and had said, "Behold, the house of Judah is like unto all the heathen" (25:8). Israel's punishment should not be the object of the Gentiles' laughter. Nor should Jehovah's people be an object of violence, although these were allowed to execute God's punishment on His rebellious people.

Part III, chapters thirty-three through forty-eight. The subject of Israel is resumed and has to do chiefly with the restoration and the future spiritual state of Israel. In the preceding chapters (25-32) the prophet pronounced judgment against the nations surrounding Judea, and he now turns to rebuke the so-called spiritual leaders within Judea — the wicked shepherds.

> And the word of Jehovah came unto me, saying, Son of man, prophesy against the shepherds of Israel, prophesy and say unto them, Thus saith the Lord God unto the shepherds: Woe be to the shepherds of Israel who shepherd themselves, should not the shepherds shepherd the sheep? Ye eat the fat and ye clothe you with the wool, ye kill them that are fed: but ye feed not the flock. . . . Behold I am against the shepherds, and I will require my flock at their hand, and cause them to cease shepherding the flock, no longer shall the shepherds feed themselves. I will rescue my sheep from their mouth, that they may not be food for them (Ezek. 34:1-3, 10).

It is here that Ezekiel gives us a picture of the Messiah under the figure of the Good Shepherd and contrasts Him with the Jewish leaders of that day who have led their people astray. Note the differences:

The wicked shepherds scattered the flock (vv. 5, 6).

The Good Shepherd will gather them (v. 13).

The false shepherds feed themselves (v. 3).

The Good Shepherd will feed his sheep (vv. 14, 15).

The false shepherds neglected the sheep (v. 4).

The Good Shepherd will seek after them and deliver them (vv. 12, 14).

The parable closes with the promise that *Jehovah*, the faithful shepherd of Israel, will recover His scattered flock and care for them. The shepherd is called both Jehovah (34:11,

30, 31) and David (34:23, 24). This is in line with the prophetic utterances in other parts of the Bible that are distinctly Messianic and closely related to the Davidic Covenant:

"And it shall come to pass, when thy days be expired that thou must go to be with thy fathers, that I will raise up thy seed after thee, which shall be of thy sons, and I will establish his kingdom" (I Chron. 17:11).

"Behold, the days come, saith the Lord, that I will raise unto David a righteous branch, and a King shall reign and prosper, and shall execute judgment and justice in the earth" (Jer. 23:5).

"They shall serve Jehovah their God, and David their king, whom I will raise up unto them" (Jer. 30:9).

> The children of Israel shall abide many days without a king and without a prince, without a sacrifice and without an image, and without an ephod and teraphim. Afterward shall the children of Israel return and seek the Lord their God, and David their King, and shall fear the Lord and His goodness in the latter days (Hos. 3:4, 5).

David, in these passages, is evidently a prophetic name of the Messiah of whom the shepherd king was a type. In this some of the Jewish rabbis agree. *The Targum*, Aramaic translation of the Bible, has it, "Afterwards shall the children of Israel return and seek the help of Jehovah, and shall be obedient to the Messiah the son of David their king."

Iben Ezra, the well-known Jewish commentator of the Spanish Period, also makes Hosea 3:5 Messianic. "David, their king," says he, "this is the Messiah, the same of whom it is said, 'And My Servant David shall be a prince among them'" (Ezek. 34:23). In still another commentary, "Mezudoth David" speaks of those who will "seek the King Messiah, who comes from the seed of David, and of Him they will ask their petitions, for He shall reign over them."

The Lord Jesus likened Himself to the Good Shepherd of this parable in Ezekiel, and fully displayed all of the noble qualities and characteristics of the True Shepherd of John ten:

1. *He is the Royal Shepherd.* He is David's righteous Branch, who should reign as King and execute judgment and justice on earth. What a contrast to the wicked shepherds denounced by Jeremiah (23:1-3).

2. *He is the Divine Shepherd.* Isaiah bids us to look forward to the appearing of the Messiah and His forerunner preparing His way before Him: "O Zion, that bringest good tidings, get thee up into the high mountain; O Jerusalem, that bringest good tidings, lift up thy voice with strength; lift it up, be not afraid; say unto the cities of Judah, *Behold your God*" (Isa. 40:9).

Then he continues, "Behold, the Lord God will come with strong hand and His arm shall rule for him . . . He shall feed His flock like a shepherd, He shall gather the lambs with His arm, and carry them in His bosom, and shall gently lead those that are with young" (Isa. 40:10, 11).

3. *He is the Smitten Shepherd.* The Rev. E. Bender Samuel in his messages on Ezekiel says:

> There is a remarkable prediction in Zechariah 13:7 of our Lord that would be most difficult to understand without the light that the New Testament sheds on it, "Awake, O sword, against my Shepherd, and against the strong man that is my fellow, saith Jehovah of Hosts; Smite the Shepherd, and the sheep shall be scattered, and I will turn mine hand upon the little ones." How wonderful! It is Jehovah's Shepherd and the Strong Man His equal whom the sword of His justice, the same as the piercing spear thrust into the Savior's side (Zech. 12:10; John 19:34-37), smote and opened a fountain unto the house of David and the inhabitants of Jerusalem for sin and uncleanness (Zech. 12:1).

Christ was the Messianic Shepherd prophesied, the Good Shepherd who came to recover His sheep and in connection with this restoration a new covenant is established, "a covenant of peace, that will cause the evil beasts to cease out of the land: and they shall dwell safely in the wilderness, and sleep in the woods" (Ezek. 34:25).

DANIEL

The Book of Daniel, like its author in his day, is much spoken against in our day. The attack on the book began with Porphyry, a heathen philosopher of the third century, who wrote much against Christianity and considered Daniel as spurious, saying it was written in the times of Antiochus Epiphanes, namely, the second century B. C. He had no following in the Early Church, but in modern times Porphyry's views have been accepted by many of the Biblical scholars, especially among those who with him "think that predictive prophecy was impossible." The two most generally accepted views of the authorship and date of the Book of Daniel are:

I. That the book, as it now stands, was written and compiled either by Daniel himself or by someone else, possibly early during the Persian domination of the East (538-331 B. C.).

II. That it was composed, as held by Porphyry and his modern followers, in the times of, and in full view of, the persecutions and desecrations of Antiochus Epiphanes (168-165 B.C.).

Only the briefest outline of some of the arguments supporting the genuineness and authenticity of the Book of Daniel can here be given.

A. It is now generally admitted that Daniel was a historical character. Ezekiel whose authenticity is practically unquestioned, speaks of Daniel as a man of great wisdom, faith and righteousness, and puts him in the same category with Job and Noah. The book itself claims to contain what Daniel suffered, and saw, and heard, and received from the revealing angel. In it we find such phrases as, "I saw in the night visions"; "I, Daniel, alone saw the vision"; "I, Daniel, understood the books," etc. Are these statements true? Are they false? Does the writer lie? He would be reckless indeed who would impeach the author's veracity, or charge him with forgery.

The admission of the Book of Daniel into the Canon of the Old Testament is evidence of its historical credibility. The Jews of that time exercised extraordinary care in this matter. To them were committed the oracles of God; and whatever neglect may be laid to their charge in other matters, they were scrupulously faithful in receiving and transmitting as Holy Scripture only such documents as were certified to them as oracles of God.

B. Josephus relates that the prophecies of Daniel were shown to Alexander the Great about 300 B.C. by the high priest Jaddua, and says that the Greek monarch was greatly pleased and encouraged by the prophecy concerning the overthrow of the Persian monarchy, which seemed so clearly to refer to himself. The conqueror was so delighted that he offered to confer any favors on the Jews.

C. The evidence derived from the Apocryphal books supports the same truth. The first book of the Maccabees contains many references to Daniel. In chapter 1:54, the writer evidently looks upon Daniel's statement concerning the "abomination of desolation" as a description of the events which were connected with Antiochus Epiphanes. In chapter 2: 59, 60, he represents the dying Mattathias as exhorting his sons to be faithful in their resistance to the idolater (165 to 160 B.C.). Having cited the examples of Abraham, Joseph, Caleb, David and Elias, he points to the deliverance of Daniel's three companions from the fiery furnace, and of Daniel himself from the lion's den, for the purpose of inspiring them with patriotic courage and zeal. The historical credibility of I Maccabees is beyond dispute.

D. The New Testament is in full accord with the entire mass of evidence to which attention has been called. It treats the Book of Daniel as genuine, and accords to it historical credibility. The Lord Jesus puts His seal to the reality of

Daniel's official character as a prophet, and to the truth of his predictions (Matt. 24:15). The Book of Revelation is to a great extent a reflex of it. Its author John had certainly been powerfully impressed by the prophecies of Daniel. The title "Son of Man," which was used several times by Christ concerning Himself, and which was later on ascribed to Him by the first martyr, Stephen, was evidently taken from the Book of Daniel (Acts 7:56). The deliverances from the fiery furnace and the lion's den are referred to as actual historical occurrences (Heb. 11:33, 34). Elsewhere Paul declares that the saints shall judge the world, and his description of the antichrist seems to repeat almost literally what Daniel had prophesied (I Cor. 6:2; II Thess. 2:3-10). Sir Isaac Newton correctly stated the case when he said, "Whosoever rejects the prophecies of Daniel does as much as if he undermined the Christian religion, which, so to speak, is founded on Daniel's prophecies of Christ."

The book differs from other prophetic writings, not only in the design and objects of the messages contained in it, but also from the viewpoint of the messages themselves. The message of the great prophets from Amos to Jeremiah was: "Repent, O Israel, for the day of Jehovah's judgment is near, when the hand of a foreign power will desolate your land and carry you into captivity because of your sins." The message of Daniel was: "Be patient, and not despairing, watch and be ready, for the day of Jehovah's judgment is near, when He will overthrow the foreign oppressors of Israel, and give to the righteous remnant and to Zion, His choice and pride, the glory and power promised from of old." It is this fact that stamps the prophecies with the peculiar features that the book exhibits.

There is no difficulty in analyzing this book and it may be studied as a highly interesting sermon on the text in four words in chapter 4:26, "the heavens do rule." This fundamental truth finds varied expression and illustration both in the narratives and in the prophetic visions which make this book unique among the writers of the Old Testament.

The first chapter furnishes an invaluable lesson of conscientious self-denial, assuring us that God honors personal abstinence in matters of eating and drinking, when such habits are grounded in religious principles. "Daniel purposed in his heart that he would not defile himself with the king's dainties, nor with the wine which he drank; therefore he requested of the prince of the eunuchs that he might not defile himself" (v. 8). The same instruction was given to the followers of Jesus in Paul's first letter to the Corinthians:

> Concerning therefore the eating of things sacrificed to idols, we know that no idol is anything in the world, and that there is no God but one. . . . Wherefore, if meat causeth my brother to stumble, I will eat no flesh for evermore, that I cause not my brother to stumble (I Cor. 8:4, 13).

The third chapter has for more than two thousand years been a monumental object lesson of God's power to deliver his faithful servants from malignant and fiery persecution. Nebuchadnezzar set up an image in the plain of Dura and demanded for it universal homage. Three Hebrew captives, on refusing to comply with the king's decree, are cast into the fiery furnace and miraculously rescued. The experience of the immortal triumvirate, Shadrach, Meshach and Abednego and the one who LIKE A SON OF THE GODS[3] walking with the three Hebrews in the midst of the fire (Dan. 3:25), is a reminder of the divine assurance of His protection promised in Isaiah: "When thou passest through the waters, I will be with thee: when thou walkest through the fire, thou shalt not be burned, neither shall the flame kindle upon thee" (Isa. 43:2).

Another experience of a marvelous deliverance is recorded in *chapter six* in connection with the decree of Darius the

---

[3] "Like a son of the gods." The Aramaic word for "gods" is *elkin*. It is not exactly equivalent to *Elohim in the Hebrew*. Daniel, though a monotheist, did not attempt to alter the incorrect, polytheistic phraseology of Nebuchadnezzar, but preserved a true record.

Mede, which caused Daniel to be thrown into the den of lions. This deliverance from the den of lions is an impressive and memorable picture of the presence and power of "the angel of the Lord[4] who encampeth round about them that fear him and delivereth them" (Ps. 34:7). It reminds us of Paul's experience and testimony:

> At my first defence no one took my part, but all forsook me: may it not be laid to their account. But the Lord stood by me, and strengthened me; that through me the message might be fully proclaimed, and that all the Gentiles might hear: and I was delivered out of the mouth of the lion (II Tim. 4:16, 17).

Nebuchadnezzar's proclamation in *chapter four* of his conversion to the King of Heaven, following his vision of the tree which filled all the earth, and of his loss of reason until "seven times" passed over him, is admirably adapted to extol the wisdom, power and glory of the one True God (v. 37). It is remarkable when we think of what power the king had, who was wont to boast on more than one occasion, "Is not this great Babylon, that I have built for the house of the kingdom by the might of my power, and for the honor of my majesty?" (v. 30)

The *second chapter* carries an impressive illustration of the statement in the prophecy of Amos (3:7), "that the Lord Jehovah will do nothing, except reveal His secret unto his servants the prophets." The vision of the kingdom of God in this chapter and from the lessons in the *fifth chapter* brings us face to face with "the God of gods, and the Lord of lords who reveals secrets."

We shall note the next six chapters of visions only in outline. *Chapter seven* is a vision, in the first year of Belshazzar, of four beasts symbolizing four world powers. *Chapter*

---

4 "The angel of the Lord." Daniel said, "My God hath sent his angel, and hath shut the lions' mouths . . ." and Nebuchadnezzar said, "Blessed be the Lord of Shadrach, Meshach, and Abednego, who hath sent His Angel and delivered His servants," so that the "Son of God" and "His Angel" are but two names for the fourth One in the furnace. The rabbis, according to Kimchi, say: "The Lord he is King Messiah, and He is the Angel of the Covenant."

eight, in the third year of Belshazzar, is a vision of a ram
with two horns and a he-goat. Daniel's great prayer for his
people in the *ninth chapter* is a model of humble confession
and earnest supplication. The angelology of chapters ten
through twelve, is a revelation of the infinite resources and
manifold agencies God uses to rule and reign in the heavens
and upon the earth, and working signs and wonders everywhere.

No less impressive are the Messianic messages found in the
Book of Daniel. In these chapters several Messianic titles are
found: the "Son of Man" (7:13), the "Prince" in chapters
eight and ten, also the "Prince of the host," "the Prince of
princes" and "Messiah the Prince." The title "Son of Man"[5]
had Messianic meaning in the literature between the testaments, and was used by our Lord Himself as a title indicating
His Messiahship. In such passages as Matthew 25:31 and
Mark 14:62, our Lord uses it as a practical equivalent of
Son of God, since He uses it in connection with the exercise
of His divine prerogatives. In the Book of Daniel with which
our Lord was well acquainted, and from which He quoted,
the Messianic and divine nature of the Son of Man is indicated, for "His dominion is an everlasting dominion, which
shall not pass away, and His kingdom that which shall not be
destroyed" (Dan. 7:14).

The "Prince" called the "prince of the Host," "the prince
of princes" and "Messiah the Prince" (8:11 and 9:25) is
"under authority" as well as having authority over others.

---

[5] In one form or another the name "Son of man" is used of Christ eight
times in Daniel, so it is His most prominent name in the book. In chapter
seven, "there came with the clouds of heaven one like unto the son of man
. . . and there was given Him dominion . . . and judgment was given to
the saints." In chapters eight and twelve "the man was clothed in linen . . .
above the waters" "between the banks of the river." In chapter nine Daniel
had confessed his and his people's sins, and Gabriel came to tell him of
expiating and redeeming judgment, of "an end of sins." In chapter ten
Daniel fell at his feet and confessed his "corruption" and weakness and
three times "a hand" of "One likeness of the sons of men touched" him in
purifying judgment and strengthened him.

Here a quotation from the great Christian scholar, Dr. R. D. Wilson, is most appropriate:

> Daniel 9:25, 26 is one of the two Old Testament passages where the expected Saviour of Israel is called Messiah. The verses read: "Know therefore and understand that from the going forth of the commandment to restore and to build Jerusalem unto the Messiah the Prince shall be seven weeks: and threescore and two weeks: the street shall be built again, and the wall, even in troublous times. And after three score and two weeks shall Messiah be cut off, but not for himself..." In 8:25 the king in fierce countenance is represented as standing up "against the Prince of princes." In 2:34, 45, the deliverer is likened to a stone cut out without hands that smote and broke in pieces the image of iron and clay. In 3:25, he may possibly be the Son of God thus spoken. In 7:13, he is likened to a son of man and comes to the Ancient of Days and is given dominion and glory and a kingdom which shall not pass away. It is possible, also, that Michael the prince of 10:21 and the Michael of 12:1 is none other than the Messiah Himself.

The history of the world is centered in the great empires which have arisen in ancient times: Assyria, Babylon, Medo-Persia, the Hellenic Empire and last, Rome with all that follows. The kingdoms of the world are according to their true nature *bestial*. Therefore these kingdoms are described as beasts out of the depths of the sea and how well acquainted we are with them in our own day. Judgment is held over the great empires of this world. They have been found unfaithful in their stewardship and they receive their doom. Another king is to take their place, and rule this world. Who is this King?

A. His origin is in heaven.

B. Yet He is like the Son of Man.

C. He receives all power and dominion.

D. He is to establish the kingdom of God on earth with a citizenship of the saints of the Most High.

Daniel's return from the Babylonian captivity was a journey toward the fulfillment of the covenant hope in the coming of the Anointed Prince (Moshiach, the son of David).

These are just some of the lessons from this great book of Daniel which we should take to heart. God's love for His people and His eternal purpose to deliver them from evil are conspicuous throughout. Let no one who knows and loves the Lord fear in times of trouble. This world is yet to become His Kingdom and then it will be a just world, a world populated by men and women of all nations who have been redeemed by the precious blood of the Lamb.

In all the Messianic passages of these three prophets, Jeremiah, Ezekiel and Daniel, the dominant note is the coming of a promised and long expected person. Our rabbis of old had certainly captured the spirit of the Old Testament when they said, "All the prophets prophesied only unto the days of the Messiah" (Berach. 34b).

HAGGAI

"The destruction of the Chaldean empire (558 B.C.) and the erection of the Persian in its stead," says Dr. Charles Augustus Briggs, "was a wonderful divine interposition on behalf of the chosen people."[6] So it was. The long exile was about to come to an end. The promises of God through the prophets Isaiah, Jeremiah and Daniel were about to be fulfilled. Babylon fell and Cyrus the Great issued in about 536 B.C. the following proclamation:

> Thus saith Cyrus, king of Persia, All the kingdoms of the earth hath Jehovah, the God of heaven, given me; and he hath charged me to build him an house in Jerusalem, which is in Judah. Who is there among all his people? His God be with him, and let him go up to Jerusalem, which is in Judah, and build the house of Jehovah, the God of Israel (he is the God), which is in Jerusalem. And whosoever is left, in any place where he sojourneth, let the men of his place help him with silver and gold and with goods, and with beasts, besides the free will offering for the house of God which is in Jerusalem (Ezra 1:2-4).

More than 42,000 Jews, accompanied by 7,337 servants and 200 singers, responded to that challenge and prepared to re-

[6] *Messianic Prophecy*, p. 428.

turn to their land. Psalm one hundred twenty-six must have been the song the marchers sang:

> When the Lord turned again the captivity of Zion,
> We were like them that dream.
> Then was our mouth filled with laughter,
> And our tongue with singing:
> Then said they among the heathen,
> The Lord hath done great things for us;
> Whereof we are glad,
> Turn again our captivity, O Lord,
> As the streams in the south.
> They that sow in tears shall reap in joy.
> He that goeth forth and weeping, bearing precious seed,
> Shall doubtless come again with rejoicing, bringing his sheaves
> with him.

But the people who returned from exile found much to discourage them. Adversaries appeared from all sides to discourage them every step of the way. After a period of work on the Temple they had to give it up. The old men who remembered the glories of Solomon's Temple wept, while the people around them "weakened the hand of the people of Judah, and troubled them in building" (Ezra 4:4). No doubt many of those who returned wished they had never left Babylon. It was then that God sent His prophet Haggai, urging them to return to their neglected temple-building. His message to Zerubbabel, who was governor of Judah, stands out as a challenge to believe God:

> Yet now be strong, Zerubbabel, saith the Lord; be strong, O Joshua, son of Josedech, the high priest; and be strong, all ye people of the land, saith the Lord, and work: for I am with you, saith the Lord of hosts: According to the word that I covenanted with you when you came out of Egypt, so my Spirit remaineth among you: fear not (Hag. 2:4, 5).

In the New Testament we find the apostle Paul reminding the Corinthian Christians to "be strong, unmovable, always abounding in the work of the Lord, for as much as ye know that your labor is not in vain in the Lord" (I Cor. 15:58).

The prophet had to take his stand against the pessimistic views that have shown up again and again. We find in his second and fourth messages encouraging promises for their time and Messianic promises for the future.

> Yet once, it is a little while, and I will shake the heavens, and the earth, and the sea, and the dry land; and I will shake all nations, and *the desire*[7] of all nations shall come: and I will fill this house with glory, saith the Lord of 'hosts. The glory of this latter house shall be greater than of the former, saith the Lord of hosts: and in this place will I give peace, saith the Lord of hosts (Hag. 2:6-9).

The words "desire of all nations" have been given several interpretations. The rendering above is the literal sense of the Hebrew. *Hemdath* is referred by the Vulgate, Luther, the Authorized Version, and most of the older interpreters — to the Messiah as the desire of all nations. Reason to doubt the accuracy of this view is found in the singular form of the noun, attributed to the fact that the early Sofrim, scribes and copyists held to the singular, or personal meaning. The personal conception is favored by the coming of the greater glory to the latter temple. This is undoubtedly the idea conveyed by the words of the prophecy, "In this place will I give peace" which carries the mind back to David's and Isaiah's Prince of Peace promised now by Haggai to bring glory to the latter house. The real glory of even the first Temple did not consist in the grand structure, or in the gold and silver with which it was enriched, but in the cloud of the symbolical presence of God which dwelt between the cherubim. As a matter of fact, "the glory," a technical expression in Hebrew having reference only to "the glory of Jehovah," which at the dedication, "filled the house of Jehovah" (Ex. 40:34-36; I Kings 8:10, 11), was "greater" in the second Temple. Though God never honored the house with

---

[7] American Standard Version: "The precious things"; Revised Standard Version: "The treasures of all nations"; American-Jewish Translation: "The choicest things of all nations."

the five missing things mentioned in the Talmud,[8] yet when He in whom dwelleth the fullness of the Godhead bodily, and in whose face can indeed be seen "the light of the knowledge of the glory of God," came "suddenly" according to prediction (Mal. 3:1), He appeared in this very temple, and purged it and consecrated it by calling it His "Father's house" (Matt. 21:12. 13; John 2:16). There was the real Presence; there was the "greater glory."

It is not fancy or speculation on our part to regard the Tabernacle or Temple as typical. In the New Testament we are expressly told that they were "ensamples and shadows of heavenly things" (Heb. 8:5), and we should lose a great amount of spiritual truth if we did not regard them as such.

Haggai closes with one more message, chapter 2:21-23. It is a message to Zerubbabel, the royal prince of the house of David. There is to be another shaking of the nations, when the kingdoms and the armies will be overthrown. Zerubbabel, heir to the throne of David, is used here as a type of the Messiah. "I will make thee as a signet; for I have chosen thee, saith the Lord of hosts." Grace here reverses the woes pronounced against Zerubbabel's grandfather, Jehoiachin (Jer. 22:24). The promise here looks beyond Zerubbabel to Him who alone is the "express image of His person and upholding all things by the word of His power, when He had made purification of sins, sat down at the right hand of the Majesty on high" (Heb. 1:3).

ZECHARIAH

Zechariah was a contemporary of Haggai and, like him, was sent to encourage the people in their work of temple building and national restoration. Of the prophet himself we know little except that which can be gathered from the book.

[8] The Talmud speaks of five things that were missing in the second Temple and which were found in the first. These are: (1) The Ark, i.e., the Mercy-Seat of the cherubim; (2) the fire from heaven upon the altar; (3) the visible Presence; (4) the Holy Spirit, and (5) the Urim and Thummim (*Yoma.* fol. 21, col. 2).

Zechariah (Heb. "Jehovah remembers") is the son of Berechiah and the grandson of Iddo who, according to Nehemiah (12:4-16), was one of the priests who left Babylon and went with Zerubbabel to Jerusalem around 536 B.C. It would, therefore, appear that Zechariah was a priest as well as a prophet, that he was born in Babylonia, and as a young man (naar), may have known Daniel as well as Haggai and now, two months after Haggai began to preach, the word of Jehovah came to Zechariah "in the second year of Darius," 520 B.C.

The historical setting of the book consists of four addresses of unequal length. These are:

I. *The Call to Repentance* (ch. 1:1-6). This is the introduction and serves to introduce the theme of the entire book: "The Lord has been sore displeased with your fathers. Therefore say thou unto them, Thus saith the Lord of hosts; turn ye unto me, saith the Lord of hosts . . . turn ye now from your evil doings: but they did not hear, nor harken unto me, saith the Lord . . ." (Zech. 1:2-4). This is not only an introduction to the theme of the book, but also a kind of inspired resumé of one great part of the work of "the former prophets" — their never-ceasing plea, "Repent."

II. *The Series of Eight Visions of Symbolic Value* (ch. 1:6 to end of ch. 6), all of which was to encourage the people at work on the Temple, leading up to the "last days," and to the *finale* of God's dealings with Israel and the nations. There are two passages that should be considered together:

> Hear now, O Joshua the high priest, thou and thy fellows that sit before thee; for they are men which are wondered at (men of miracle): for, behold, I will bring forth my servant the Branch. For, behold, the stone that I have set before Joshua; upon one stone shall be seven eyes: behold, I will engrave the graving thereof, saith the Lord of hosts, and I will remove the iniquity of that land in one day. In that day, saith the Lord of hosts, shall ye call every man his neighbor under the vine and under the fig tree (Zech. 3:8-10).

The words "My servant the Branch" take us back to Isaiah who first used these figures Messianically. "In that day shall the Branch (Tsemach) of the Lord be beautiful and glorious, and the fruit of the earth shall be excellent and comely . . ." (Isa. 4:2). A land that was desolate and cursed because of its sins will "in that day," when Messiah comes, put forth a new and beautiful sprout (Tsemach) to wash away "the filth of the daughter of Zion, and shall have purged the blood of Jerusalem from the midst thereof" (Isa. 4:4). This is Isaiah's picture of generated life in the Messianic Age. This new life is further revealed in Isaiah 11:1 through the offspring of David, a sprout from the stock of Jesse. Then Jeremiah (ch. 25 and 28), and Zechariah (3:8; 6:12) took up the same term to give more definite and personal expression. Thus "My Servant," the title of the Messiah in the second half of the prophecy of Isaiah, takes our minds back to the familiar verses of Isaiah 42:1-6, 49:6.

The second passage under consideration is found in Zechariah six:

> And the word of the Lord came unto me, saying, Take them of the captivity, even of Heldai, or Tobijah, and of Jedaiah, which are come from Babylon, and come thou the same day, and go to the house of Josiah, the son of Zephaniah; then take silver and gold, and make crowns, and set them upon the head of Joshua, the son of Josedech, the high priest; and speak unto him, saying, Thus speaketh the Lord of hosts, saying, Behold the man whose name is Branch; and he shall grow up out of his place, and shall build the temple of the Lord; even he shall build the temple of the Lord; and he shall bear the glory, and shall sit and rule upon the throne; and he shall be a priest upon his throne; and the counsel of peace shall be between them both. And the crown shall be to Helem, and to Tobijah, and to Jedaiah and to Hen, the son of Zephaniah, for a memorial in the temple of the Lord. And they that are far off shall come and build in the temple of the Lord, and ye shall know that the Lord of hosts hath sent me unto you. And this shall come to pass, if ye will willingly obey the voice of the Lord your God (Zech. 6:9-15).

This is perhaps the most remarkable Messianic prophecy in the Old Testament as to the person of the promised Redeemer, the office He was to fill and the mission He was to accomplish. The person here described is to be both priest and king, and there is to be no discord between the two offices in one person. "Behold the Man"—these words used by God Himself, are addressed to Joshua, as a type of a coming person. It is idle speculation to say that this was written of Simon or John Hyrcanus, who were priest-rulers (170-135 B.C.); for the passage is a genuine part of the book. Nor is there anything to explain why Joshua's name should be used for Simon or John Hyrcanus. We are aware of the fact that such Jewish commentators as Rashi, Iben Ezra and Kimchi assert that "the Man, the Branch," is Zerubbabel; but for obvious controversial reasons, these men have departed from the older received interpretations, as seen from Targum Jonathan,[9] where the passage (verse 12) is paraphrased thus: "Behold the Man; Messiah is His Name. He will be revealed, and He will become great and build the Temple of God." The Messianic interpretation is held by Abrabanel, the Jerusalem Talmud (Ber.. 5a), in Pirke de R. Eliezer and in the Midrashim. As in psalm one hundred ten, we have here again the conception of the Messiah as Priest and King.

Of this passage Dr. Alexander McCaul says, "The prophecy promises three particulars: first, He shall be a priest upon His throne; secondly, He shall build the Temple of the Lord; thirdly, He shall bear the glory,[10] and shall sit and rule upon the throne, and they that are far off shall come and build the temple of the Lord."[11] It is easy to identify these features in the character of Jesus of Nazareth. As to the question asked,

[9] He was a pupil of Hillel, at the beginning of the Christian century, but the Targum in its present form is of about the fifth century A.D. See also David Baron's *Visions and Prophecies of Zechariah*, p. 191.

[10] The Hebrew word *hod* strictly denotes the majesty of a king.

[11] Dr. Alexander McCaul, a great Hebrew scholar, was Professor of Divinity at King's College, London, and the author of *The Old Paths*, etc., etc.

"What Temple is it which the Messiah, according to this prophecy and other predictions, was to build?"

Says David Baron,

> In answer to this question we should say first of all that we cannot remove from the prophecy the reference to a literal Temple in Jerusalem, which shall, after Israel's national conversion, be built under the superintendence of their Messiah-King, and which will, during the millennial period, be "the House of Jehovah on earth," which is to be the central place of Millennial Worship.

III. *The Message of Reassurance* (ch. 7 and 8). It is a fourfold reply to questions asked concerning certain fasts. The answer was that the keeping of such feasts and fasts was a mere form. The fast of the fifth month (Tisha B'av, answering to July or August) is still observed by the Jews in memory of the destruction of Jerusalem and the Temple by Nebuchadnezzar in 586 B.C.[12] The Lord's answer through His prophet is described in these two chapters and closed with *devarim tovim, devarim nechamim* — "good words, even comforting words" (1:13):

> Thus saith the Lord; I am returned unto Zion, and will dwell in the midst of Jerusalem: and Jerusalem shall be called a city of truth; and the mountain of the Lord of hosts the holy mountain. Thus saith the Lord of hosts; There shall yet old men and old women dwell in the streets of Jerusalem, and every man with his staff in his hand for every age. And the streets of the city shall be full of boys and girls playing in the streets thereof. Thus saith the Lord of hosts; If it be marvellous in the eyes of the remnant of this people in these days, should it also be marvellous in mine eyes? saith the Lord of hosts. Thus saith the Lord of hosts; Behold, I will save my people from the east country, and from the west country; and I will bring them, and they shall dwell in the midst of Jerusalem: and they shall be my people, and I will be their God, in truth and in righteousness (8:3-8).

[12] Aaron Judah Kligerman, *Feasts and Fasts of Israel,* Chapter IV—"A Day of Mourning." The Talmud and some historians list a number of other calamities that happened on the Ninth of Av and among them also the destruction of the Second Temple by the Romans.

Jerusalem will become a joy of all the earth and the nations witnessing her beauty and grace will long to share with Israel in her high privilege:

> Thus saith the Lord of hosts; In those days it shall come to pass, that ten men shall take hold out of all languages of the nations, even shall take hold of the skirt of him that is a Jew, saying, We will go with you: for we have heard that God is with you (Zech. 8:23).[13]

IV. *Prophecies of the Great Messianic Future* (9:1-14:21). In this part of Zechariah there are more prophecies concerning a personal Messiah than in any other part of the Old Testament. Thus the entry of Zion's lowly King is described most vividly:

> Rejoice greatly, O daughter of Zion;
> Shout, O daughter of Jerusalem:
> Behold, thy King cometh unto thee!
> He is just and having salvation;
> Lowly, and riding on an ass,
> And upon a colt — the foal of an ass[14] (Zech. 9:9).

The King who enters Jerusalem, whom it will greet with jubilation, is a righteous one (*tsadic*), and such an one as God has helped out of affliction and struggle to redemption and victory. He has gone through a school of suffering, and is called salvation (*nosha*), the lowly one, who does not come mounted on a horse, not as the kings of the world, but as a king who is to come first to save that which is lost and in due time to reign "from sea to sea, and from the river to the ends of the earth" (Zech. 9:10b; Ps. 72:8).

When Jesus of Nazareth was about to enter Jerusalem on the first day of the Passover week (Matt. 21:1-11), He brought to pass the literal fulfillment of these words in Himself, by sending His disciples to bring the colt spoken of in this prophecy hundreds of years before. By this Jesus proclaimed Himself as Messiah. He is the only person in

---

[13] In Yalkut Shimoni, a collection of Midrashic material, we read: "All nations shall come, falling on their faces before the Messiah and the Israelites, praying, Grant that we may be Thy servants, and Israel's."

[14] One animal "an ass, that is, a colt of the ass species."

all history whose character and experience answer to this description of the Ideal King. These words have no meaning in Zechariah apart from the goal in Jesus, the true *Tsadic* — the Righteous One, the Prince who "shall speak peace to the nations."

In chapter 11:1-3 we find the prelude to a fresh prophecy:

> Open the doors, O Lebanon, that the fire may devour the cedars. Howl, fir tree; for the cedar is fallen; because the mighty are spoiled: Howl, O ye oaks of Bashan: for the forest of the vintage is come down. There is a voice of the howling of the shepherds; for their glory is spoiled: a voice of the roaring of the young lions; for the pride of Jordan is spoiled.

This is a crisis and the prophet receives a new commission to set forth the causes and the manner of the judgments which were announced in general terms in the first three verses, and to "the sheep of slaughter" (11:7). The Targum has it: "Prophecy against the rulers (of Israel) who were appointed to rule the people, but rule over them as over sheep led to the slaughter." In Ezekiel thirty-four, God speaks up against the "shepherds of Israel that do feed themselves," that He will "set up one Shepherd over them, and He shall feed them . . ." (v. 23). This is how God is always dealing with Israel, both in mercy and in judgment. It is God in the Messiah who acts, and in this book the Messianic promises are of the Christ who came to serve, to die, and to redeem man.

> And I said unto them, If ye think good, give me my price; and if not, forbear. So they weighed for my price thirty pieces of silver. And the Lord said unto me, Cast it unto the potter, the goodly price that I was priced at by them. And I took the thirty pieces of silver, and cast them unto the potter, in the house of Jehovah (Zech. 11:12, 13).

In the New Testament, Matthew cites this prophecy as fulfilled in the betrayal of our Lord Jesus when Judas sold his Lord and Master for thirty pieces of silver, which, when he returned it to the High Priest, was used to buy the potter's field (Matt. 27:9, 10).[15]

The last three chapters of the book, twelve, thirteen and fourteen, take us into the distant future. It is eschatological and apocalyptic in its character, for it is impossible to apply the predictions in these chapters to the events that took place during the destruction of Jerusalem by Nebuchadnezzar (586 B.C.), or to the destruction of the city and Temple which was to take place later on in 70 A.D. The *Yom ha'hu*, "that day" which is mentioned so often in these chapters, refers not to Messiah's first coming as the Suffering Servant of Jehovah, but to His appearance in glory. He is coming to judge the nations· as well as Israel because of their rejection of the Messiah, and when they discover their sad loss and cry for help in their distress, He pours upon them His Spirit:

> And I will pour upon the house of David, and upon the inhabitants of Jerusalem, the spirit of grace and of supplication; and they shall look unto me whom they have pierced; and they shall mourn for him, as one mourneth for an only son, and shall be in bitterness for him, as one that is in bitterness for his firstborn (Zech. 12:10).[16]

"There is nothing in the whole range of Scripture," said the late Adolph Saphir, "that is more touching than the promise contained in these simple, unadorned words. As they touch the heart they fix themselves on our memory. Who can ever forget them? 'They shall look upon me whom they have pierced.'"

When in God's own time· this happens, it will be Israel's New· Birth, the birthday of a whole nation "born at once" (Isa. 66:8). "In that day" we are told —

[15] Matthew's statement that Jeremiah spoke these words is not a slip of the pen nor a scribal error, but "because he wished to impress upon his readers the fact of Zechariah's prediction of two fearful prophecies and was a reiteration of the prophecies of Jeremiah (chs. 18, 19). This seems to be the view held by Drs. McCaul and Edersheim.

[16] Rashi translates it: "They will turn to Me in complaint." The mourning according to most present-day Jewish commentators, is over those Jews who fell in the defense of their city as martyrs for their faith and country.

> There shall be a fountain opened to the house of David and to the inhabitants of Jerusalem, for sin and for uncleanness (Zech. 13:1).

This is in harmony with the prophecies of Ezekiel, where we find promises of Israel's Restoration (36:24), Israel's Purification (36:25), Israel's Regeneration (36:26) and finally Israel's Sanctification (36:27,28).

In the last chapter, fourteen, of this book we have a summary of the events at the return of our Lord, and in this instance, it is the coming of the Messiah in glory to set up His kingdom on earth. Zechariah's vision of the future kingdom is excelled only by the New Testament prophet, the apostle John, who on the Isle of Patmos recorded his visions of things to come — "When at evening time it shall be light . . . and the Lord shall be King over all the earth: in that day shall there be one LORD and his name one" (Zech. 14:7,9).

MALACHI

Malachi — "My Messenger" — is the name of the last book of the Old Testament. Malachi was the last messenger of the Old Testament Dispensation. When the echo of his prophetic message died away there was a silence for the period of four hundred years; four hundred years before a note will be sounded which is important enough to be placed within the covers of the Old Testament Canon.

The personality or identity of Malachi is unknown beyond the simple superscription in the opening verses of the book. He, like many of his predecessors, was a burden bearer: "The burden of the word of the Lord to Israel by Malachi" (1:1). There are some who do not regard the name Malachi as a proper name, but, says Dr. Charles A. Briggs, "There seem to be no sufficient reasons for rejecting Malachi as a proper name for the prophet, and exegetical opinion has turned strongly in favor of this interpretation."[17] We believe that

---

[17] *Messianic Prophecy*, p. 472.

the author of the book was Malachi and that he was the messenger of Jehovah. All the other prophetical books, even the short ones as Obadiah, Nahum and Haggai, bear the names of their authors. It is unlikely that the last book of the Old Testament would be anonymous.

The message of the book is divided into three sections with the introductory assurance of God's love for Israel (1:1-5).

Section I is a message of rebuke against the priests who have dishonored their Lord: "A son honoreth his father, and a servant his master; if then I be a father, where is Mine honor? and if I be a master, where is My fear? saith the Lord of hosts unto you, O priests, that despise My name" (see 1:6-2:9).

Section II, is a rebuke of the people as well as the priests for the utter confusion in their social life, and for their unfaithfulness in their marriage relations. Intermarriage with the surrounding heathens was an abomination to the God who appointed them to be a Holy Nation (2:10-16). This was the same burden and complaint of Ezra:

> The princes came to me, saying, The people of Israel, and the priests, and the Levites, have not separated themselves from the people of the lands, doing according to their abominations, even of the Canaanites, the Hittites, the Perizzites, the Jebusites, the Ammonites, the Moabites, the Egyptians, and the Amorites. For they have taken of their daughters for themselves, and for their sons: so that the holy seed have mingled themselves with the people of those lands: yea, the hand of the princes and rulers hath been chief in this trespass (Ezra 9:1-2).

And Nehemiah adds his own observations:

> In those days also saw I Jews that hath married wives of Ashdod, of Ammon, and of Moab: and their children spake half in the speech of Ashdod, and could not speak the Jews' language, but according to the language of each people (Neh. 13:23, 24).

Section III, is a series of prophecies concerning the Advent of the Lord and is therefore Messianic (2:17-4:6).

The first Messianic passage of the book tells of a messenger whose mission it is to introduce the One who has been "the desire of all nations" (Hag. 2:7) and Israel's great Hope.

> Behold, I send my messenger, and he shall prepare the way before me: and the Lord whom ye seek, shall suddenly come to His temple, even the Messenger of the Covenant, whom ye delight in: Behold, he shall come, saith the Lord of hosts (Mal. 3:1).

The One expected here, *Ha-adon*, "the Lord whom ye seek," must be divine in nature, for the "messenger" (Malachi), who is to prepare the way of the Lord is explained in Malachi 4:5, as a second Elijah, a great prophet, who is an appropriate type of Elijah the Tishbite (II Kings 1:8). He, the *Ha-adon*, who will come suddenly, is also the "Messenger of the Covenant," the Malach-Habrith, promised to the fathers and prophets. It is the same Angel-Presence who appeared in the days of the patriarchs and to Israel throughout their history. It has pleased God to make Himself known in general Revelation, but it pleased Him to make Himself known in a more special sense, in which He is pleased to enter into the limits of the sphere of the creature, in order to present Himself personally and to give testimony of Himself to man. The forms and vehicles in which this divine self-presentation and self-witness reaches man from without are:

1. *Through the Voice*, (*Bat Kol*) — "While the word was in the king's mouth, there fell a voice from heaven, saying, O king Nebuchadnezzar, to thee it is spoken; the kingdom is departed from thee" (Dan. 4:31). We meet the same Voice in the New Testament: "And lo a voice from heaven, saying, This is my beloved Son, in whom I am well pleased" (Matt. 3:17).[18]

2. *Through the Angel*, (Malach). An acquaintance with this unique Person as revealed in the Bible in such passages as Genesis 18:1, 2; 21:17, 18; 22:11; 28:10-22; 32:24; 48:15, 16; Exodus 2:24, 25; 3:2; 14:19; Numbers 20:16; Hosea 12:4,

---

[18] The rabbis say that upon the death of the last of the prophets, "the Holy Spirit departed from Israel," but, they add, "resort was had to the Bat Kol" (Sanhedrin 11a, Yoma 9b).

etc., leads to the conclusion that in Him we see none other than the Second Person of our Triune God.[19]

3. *Through the Shekinah* (The Presence). "The Presence" is frequently used in the Talmud and Midrash as a name for God. The name Shekinah is used as a name for God only when the rabbis speak of God's nearness to man. "Whenever Israel is enslaved, Shekinah, as it were, is enslaved with them . . . 'In all their affliction He was afflicted' (Isa. 63:9)."[20] Again: "When Israel went down to Egypt, Shekinah went down with them, as it says, 'I will go down with thee into Egypt' (Gen. 46:4); when they went into the wilderness, Shekinah was with them, as it says, 'And the Lord went before them by day' (Ex. 13:21)."[21]

This is significant, because of the lamentable tendency among our modern Jews and some Christians who think of the Holy Spirit (*Ruach hakodesh*) as a mere influence for good or some kind of energy of God. He is more than these: He is the Third Person of the Trinity. Our Lord Jesus, Israel's promised Messiah, is the Mediator between God and man; the mission of the Spirit is to reveal Christ to man.

But the most significant and satisfactory comment on this first Messianic passage in Malachi is found in one of the gospels in the New Testament:

> Behold, I send my messenger before thy face which shall prepare thy way before thee. The voice of one crying in the wilderness, Prepare ye the way of the Lord, make His paths straight (Mark 1:2, 3).

Between the time of Malachi and the announced coming of "the Messenger of the Covenant," four hundred years ran their course. During this period the promise contained in these words was the only Good News to men. What was

---

[19] Angel of the Covenant. Of this our rabbis say, "The Lord He is King Messiah and He is the Angel of the Covenant" (David Kimchi).

[20] Mekilta, I, 25; II, p. 27.

[21] Max Kadushin in his book, *The Rabbinic Mind*, has an interesting section on Revelation of Shekinah (God).

the forceful element therein? It was a word of power, the promise of the dawn of a new day, the Day of the Lord.

There is an old Jewish custom of opening the street door during the Seder on Passover night. A direct invitation is given to those who may pass by. "This is the poor bread which our fathers ate in the land of Egypt. Let any one who is hungry, come in and eat; let any one who is needy, come in and make Passover." This was written in Chaldee, because the men in the street would best understand that language in Babylon, where the Haggadah was composed. "During the Middle Ages," according to Israel Abrahams, "a sort of a faint shadow of the old custom may be caught. It became habitual to open the door on the Passover eve, at the end of the meal. This looks rather inhospitable, but the door was opened for a special guest; for Elijah, the harbinger of the Messiah."[22]

God is not abandoning the world He created. The Day of the Lord is coming with a greater than Elijah at the doors. "Unto you that fear My Name shall the Sun of Righteousness arise with healing in His wings" (Mal. 4:2).

> Arise, shine; for thy light is come, and the glory of the Lord is risen upon thee. For, behold, the darkness shall cover the earth, and gross darkness the people: but the Lord shall arise upon thee, and his glory shall be seen upon thee. . . . The sun shall be no more thy light by day; neither for brightness shall the moon give light unto thee; but the Lord shall be unto thee an everlasting light, and thy God thy glory (Isa. 60:1, 2, 19).

"The heart of the fathers toward the children?" That is the Old Testament looking toward the New. "The heart of the children toward their fathers?" That is the New Testament turning its face toward the Old. And thus has the providential preservation and order manifested in gracious beauty the meeting place between the Old and the New, the unbroken and undivided Scriptures.

[22] *Aspects of Judaism*, pp. 32, 33.

CHAPTER VIII

WE HAVE FOUND THE MESSIAH

If we were asked to glance back into the history of mankind, and distinguish one man among all the philosophers, teachers, poets, orators, statesmen and deliverers, whose character was most blameless, whose influence was most enduring and whose example was most worthy of imitation, three-fifths of the human race would designate Jesus of Nazareth as The Man. In this, Jew, Gentile and Christian will agree.

Jews were always willing to welcome truth irrespective of its source. They have learned much from Aristotle, Plato, Homer, Virgil, Milton and Tennyson, but there is one name that in the past was cast out from among the Jews. A name, despised and hated, and yet, a name that represents the founder of a religion that has drawn about it great multitudes of all sorts and kinds of people all over the world. Jesus of Nazareth, though blood, bone and flesh of the Jew, has hitherto been dreaded and shunned by the Jew.

But this hostile attitude toward Him cannot continue. Enlightened Jews of today have had to cease blaming this Man of Galilee and His Gospel for atrocities committed by pagans falsely called Christians. German Nationalism may try to make a Nordic of Him, but to the Jew of today He is one of his own. *Ante Christum* and *Anno Domini* are no longer mere arbitrary chronological distinctions to the Jew, but historical facts which cannot now be easily discarded. Whatever view the Jew may take about the person of Christ, he can not deny that with Him came "a new teaching with authority," which changed the face of the world. In spite of all the failures, and crimes, committed in His name (and they are many), the thinking Jew of today nevertheless sees that true Christianity is a progressive, expansive, cosmopolitan religion; a religion that draws its strength and inspiration from but one source alone, and that source — Jesus of Nazareth. Before the mind of the modern Jew there passes a list of twenty-four false messiahs who have arisen among his people since the destruction of the Second Temple, and who in every instance have been a curse and a calamity to those who followed them. But here is this quiet Man of Nazareth, after nineteen centuries of testing, still matchless in His character and authority and power to transform for the better all that is yielded to His control.

Three mighty men sought universal empire — Alexander, Caesar and Napoleon. Alexander lies dead, and on his gravestone is written "Failure." Caesar lies dead at the foot of Pompey's pillar, a complete failure. Napoleon with his battle flags around him, has lain for over a century a buried "Failure."

There is one and ONE ONLY who has sought universal empire and won it, not by the might and power of carnal weapons, but by the sheer power of His Holy Word and Spirit. Jesus of Nazareth is that one. The Jew of today knows all that and he is perplexed. Today as in the days of the apostles the Jew is confronted with the question, "What think ye of Christ? Who is this Man? Is He indeed the God-promised Messiah, or must we wait for another?" And as in the days of the apostles, the Jewish inquirer must be directed to the Old Testament Scriptures for a satisfactory answer.

> Within that awful volume lies
> The mystery of mysteries!
> Happiest they of human race,
> To whom the Lord has granted grace
> To read, to fear, to hope, to pray,
> To lift the latch, and force the way.[1]

[1] Walter Scott.

When the apostle Peter met the Roman centurion, Cornelius, and in brief terms traced the leading facts of the life, work and death of Christ, he added, "To Him give all the prophets witness." The apostle Peter was right. There are four hundred and fifty-six references in the Old Testament to the Messiah and Messianic times. Peter, the Jew, did what any other Bible trained and trusting Jew would do when confronted with a question regarding the Messiahship of the Man who lived, served, and died for the benefit of His fellow man. But he also followed the line of rabbinical teaching on the subject. According to the rabbis, "All the prophets prophesied only unto the days of the Messiah."[2] "The world itself was created for the Messiah."[3] He also followed the instructions of his Master, who throughout His ministry called upon His hearers to "Search the Scriptures."[4] And "the Scripture" to thousands of the first followers of the Lord Jesus Christ meant solely and exclusively the Old Testament.[5] From that Book alone could and did they come to know the Messiah.

I propose therefore in what is to follow to consider briefly the prophets, their immediate aim, their ultimate aim, and the fulfillment of their predictions.

THE PROPHETS

They were men of Israel who claimed to be the mouthpieces of Jehovah; the organs of divine communication. "Thus saith Jehovah"; "The word of Jehovah came unto me saying," etc., etc.[6] That was the message, and they sought to deliver it faithfully. In the delivery they used the style with which they had been endued. They differed greatly in intellectual endowment, training and environment, but in one point they all agreed: each was an organ of divine inspiration. How-

[2] Berach, 34b.
[3] Shabb, 63a.
[4] John 5:39.
[5] II Timothy 3:15-17; II Peter 1:21.
[6] Zechariah 7:11, 12.

ever unlike the form of utterance, what was uttered was the
Voice of the Living God.

Their Immediate Aim

They were to watch, direct, comfort[7] and rebuke. There
were times when there was "no truth, nor mercy, nor knowledge of God in the land,"[8] when the rich ground the faces
of the poor, and prosperity led to extremes of luxury and self-
indulgence. Then the true prophets of God lifted their voices
like a trumpet and delivered the message they had been entrusted by Him. Prophets like Nathan, Elijah and Isaiah
stand as living witnesses to the faithfulness and courage of
the true prophet of God. Conscious of their high calling, they
refused to bow down before any human creature. They called
upon king and peasant, rich and poor, to repent and be saved,
or the wrath of God would overtake them. To be sure, there
was also much tenderness in their message. They spoke of
God's tender mercy, of His attentiveness to the cry of the
destitute; of His patience and readiness to forgive. "How shall
I give thee up, Ephraim? How shall I deliver thee, Israel?
I will not execute the fierceness of mine anger, I will not
return to destroy Ephraim."[9]

Their Ultimate Aim

But besides this interest in the people of their own time,
there is also a definite outlook upon the future, which can
be called the ultimate aims of the prophets.

Their aim was to prepare for and aid in the establishing of
the kingdom of God on this earth. This was accomplished
in a threefold manner:

A. *They foretold the doom of existing earthly empires.*
These man-made organizations stood in the way of the kingdom of God. They represented everything that was in opposi-
tion to God's original plan for the world. Hence the severe

[7] Isaiah 40:1-10; 53; 55.
[8] Hosea 4:1.
[9] Hosea 11:8, 9.

denunciations of the prophets against Edom, Ammon and Moab. "The nation and the kingdom that will not serve thee shall perish; yea, those nations shall utterly be wasted."[10] The overthrow of the false before the erection of the true was the message of Israel's prophets.

B. *They foretold the coming of a new religion.* Isaiah and Micah represent the Mountain of the Lord's House as exalted far above all other mountains, and so attracting the attention of the nations that they in a body come and offer themselves in willing subjection to the God of Israel. Even former enemies of Israel are experiencing conversion. Assyria and Egypt, Rahab and Babylon, Tyre and Philistia register in the City of God (Ps. 87; Isa. 2:2). Thus the promise made to Abraham (Gen. 12:3), that in his seed all the nations will be blessed, is surely to come to pass.

C. *But the chief method by which the prophets sought to prepare the Way of the Lord* was by setting forth *The Person* who is to bring about the desired changes. As to His appearance in the world we have a multitude of details.

It was foretold:

1. That Messiah would be a descendant of Abraham, and of Jacob, and of the stem of Jesse (Gen. 22:18; Num. 24: 16, 17, 19; Isa. 11:1).

2. That He would come during the time of the Second Temple[11] (Hag. 2:9; Mal. 3:1).

3. That the Sceptre should not depart from Judah until Shiloh come[12] (Gen. 49:1, 10).

---

[10] Isaiah 60:12.

[11] Rav Hillel (not the Elder) says: "Israel need not expect any Messiah; for they had him already in the days of Hezekiah." (The prophecies concerning him had reference to that time.) "May the Lord forgive Rav Hillel!" exclaimed Rav Yoseph; for did not Hezekiah flourish during the first Temple? and did not Zechariah prophesy during the *second* Temple? (Zech. 9:9): 'Rejoice greatly, O daughter of Zion; behold, thy King cometh unto thee: just, and having salvation; lowly, and riding upon an ass, and upon a colt, the foal of an ass' " (Sanhed. 99a).

[12] Perhaps the most probable explanation of the word "Shiloh" is that it should be read "Sheloi." Compare Ezekiel 21:27—"until He come whose right it is." "Shiloh" is acknowledged to many Jewish writers to be the Messiah. So Onkelos, the two Jerusalem Targums, and others. See Sanhedrin 98b.

4. That His birthplace would be in Bethlehem, an obscure village in Judea (Mic. 5:2).

5. That His birth would be miraculous — conceived by the Holy Ghost, and born of a Jewish virgin,[13] and His name would be called "Emmanuel"; Son of God and Son of Man (Isa. 7:14; Dan. 3:25; 7:13; Zech. 4:6,7).

6. That He would be the Mediator of a New and Everlasting Covenant that would include the Gentiles as well as Jews (Isa. 49:6-9; Jer. 31:30-33; Zech. 9:11; Mal. 3:1).

7. That He would unite in Himself all the offices that existed among Israel — such as: Prophet (Deut. 18:15-18), Priest (Ps. 110:4), King (Isa. 33:22), Lawgiver, Judge and Redeemer.

8. That He would perform miracles (Isa. 35:5,6; 42:1-7).

9. That He would be Redeemer of both soul and body (Job 19:25,26; Ps. 17:15).

10. That He would be a light to the Gentiles and the glory of Israel (Isa. 46:13; 49:6).

11. That He would be sold for thirty pieces of silver (Zech. 11:12,13).

12. That He would be silent before His accusers (Isa. 53:7).

13. That He would be scourged and spit upon (Isa. 50:6).

14. That His body would not see corruption (Ps. 16:10).

15. That His hands and feet would be pierced (Ps. 22:16).

16. That He would be reviled (Ps. 22:7,8).

17. That He would be given gall and vinegar (Ps. 69:21).

18. That His garments would be divided (Ps. 22:18).

19. That His bones would not be broken (Ps. 34:20).

---

[13] For the meaning of the Hebrew word *Alma* it will pay the reader to look up the following references: Genesis 24:16, 43; Exodus 2:3; Psalm 68:25 (Heb. text 26); Song of Solomon 1:3; Isaiah 7:14. All of these references refer to pure maidenhood. Why then do some Jewish leaders say that "H-Alma" in Isaiah 7:14 refers to a married woman?

20. That He would be put to death and numbered among the transgressors; cut off, but not for Himself (Isa. 53:12;[14] Dan. 9:24-26).

21. That He would ascend into heaven, to be the Great High Priest and Intercessor (Ps. 2:6,7; 68:18; 110:1,4).

22. That He would come again in glory to judge the nations (Ps. 50:3-5; Ezek. 21:27; Zech. 14:1-7).

23. That His dominion would cover the earth (Ps. 22:27; 72:11; Dan. 7:13-26; Mal. 1:11).

Where is the man who can say that none of these prophecies have been fulfilled in Jesus of Nazareth? All of the New Testament biographers of Jesus were convinced that in Him the Messiah came, lived, taught, wrought mighty works, suffered, died and rose again, in literal fulfillment of the utterance made by the Old Testament Hebrew prophets. Take, for example, the reports of Peter's speeches in Acts, in which we have fine representations of the earliest Christian teaching. In his speeches Peter starts from the historical person of the Lord Jesus and from facts well known to his hearers regarding His life on earth: "Jesus of Nazareth, a man accredited to you by God through miracles and wonders and

[14] I am acquainted with rabbinic teaching denying that the fifty-third chapter of Isaiah relates to the Messiah, and that interprets it to be a picture of some of the prophets and of suffering Israel. We cannot agree to such an interpretation, because the character of the person described by Isaiah does not accord with the character of any of the prophets or of Israel as a nation.

(a) The person of Isaiah 53 was to be punished for the sins committed by others. Israel was punished for her own sins. One of our prayers makes this confession. (See *Daily Prayer Book* by Singer, page 245.)

(b) The person described in Isaiah 53 was sinless. Where is the Jew who would dare to proclaim Israel as a sinless nation?

(c) The person of Isaiah 53 submits to be slaughtered like a lamb, that is, without resistance. At no time in Israel's history have the Jews submitted tamely to their fate. Their heroism in times of war is well known to the student of Jewish history.

(d) The person of Isaiah 53 was to be cut off out of the land of the living. Israel, as a nation, still exists. Very much so! In 1825 there were 3,280,000 Jews in the world. In 1930 there were 15,800,000 Jewish souls. Isaiah 53 must apply to the Messiah. So did our rabbis believe. (Sanhed. 98b; Ber. Rabba; Pesikta Rabbathi, etc.)

signs which God performed by Him among you, as you yourselves know" (Acts 2:22); "anointed with the Holy Ghost and with power: who went about doing good, and healing all that were oppressed of the devil; for God was with Him" (Acts 10:38).

This also was the burden of Stephen's long address before his martyrdom; also of Philip when he met the eunuch reading from the Book of Isaiah; and of Paul throughout all his missionary journeys. The author of the Epistle to the Hebrews makes continuous application of the priestly functions and prophetic utterances of the Old Testament to the Lord Jesus Christ. And the apostle John, in the last book of the New Testament, makes this significant declaration: "The testimony of Jesus is the spirit of prophecy" (Rev. 19: 10).

It is clear, without a shadow of a doubt, that the writers of the New Testament and the great number of followers of the Nazarene, viewed the correspondence between the Old Testament and the New, not as a series of undesigned coincidences, or as a result of wonderful human foresight of what was to come, but as showing that each was part and parcel of one entire self-revelation of God. The Old Testament Gospel is that, "All we have gone astray; we have turned every one to his own way; and the Lord hath laid on Him the iniquity of us all . . ." (Isa. 53:6).

The glorious Gospel of the New Testament is: "If any man sin, we have an advocate with the Father, Jesus Christ, the righteous. He is the propitiation for our sins" (I John 2:1, 2).

The Old Testament Gospel is: "Ho, every one that thirsteth, come ye to the waters, and he that has no money, hearken diligently unto me, and eat that which is good. Incline your ear and come . . ." (Isa. 55:1-3). The New Testament Gospel is: "Come unto Me, all ye that labor and are heavy laden, and I will give you rest" (Matt. 11:28).

THE LORD JESUS CHRIST OUR ONLY HOPE

Our post-Biblical history is full of great leaders. I think of the aged priest Mattathias with his five stalwart sons, the Maccabees (142 B.C.); of the gentle Rabbi Hillel (75 B.C.); of Rabbi Akiba, who hailed Bar-Kochba as the promised "Star of Jacob" and who died a martyr's death for God and his country (135 A.D.); of Saadiah ben Joseph, one of the Geonim (892 A.D.); of Moses ben Maimon, commentator and philosopher and called by many "second Moses" (1135 A.D.); of Moses Mendelssohn, father of modern Judaism (1729); of Karl Marx, the great Socialist (1818); of Theodore Herzl (1860-1904), the father of Political Zionism and I ask, which of these our great leaders could we rightly acclaim as satisfying, or having satisfied our people's long deferred hope? Which of these has been the means of rekindling our slumbering fires of devotion to God, or of inflaming our souls with a divine and noble passion for the salvation of mankind? Alas, our leaders have divided and subdivided our nation until we have become a camp of "Isms."[15] The farther we drifted from the historic Messiah, the farther away we moved alike from our National Hope, and from the divine ideals of the Bible.

The great Hebrew Christian statesman, Benjamin Disraeli, known as Lord Beaconsfield, once said:

> The pupil of Moses may ask himself, whether all the princes of the house of David have done so much for the Jews as the prince who was crucified on Calvary. Had it not been for Him, the Jews would have been comparatively unknown, or known only as a high oriental caste which had lost its country. Has not He made their history the most famous in the world? Has not He hung up their laws in every temple? Has He not vindicated all their wrongs? Has He not avenged the victory of Titus and conquered the Caesars? What successes did they anticipate from their Messiah? The wildest dreams of their

[15] I have in mind the following divisions within Israel: Orthodox, Reform, and Conservative, Chassidism and Mithnagdim; Zionism, Socialism and Communism.

rabbis have been far exceeded. . . . Christians may continue to persecute Jews and Jews may persist in disbelieving Christians, but who can deny that Jesus of Nazareth, the Incarnate Son of the Most High God, is the eternal glory of the Jewish race?[16]

What then is our hope? Our hope is in Jesus of Nazareth, and in Him alone, for this is He of whom Moses and all the prophets wrote! He is the Lamb of God that taketh away the sins of the world. He is the Prince of Peace, the King of Israel, the Lord our Righteousness, King of kings and Lord of lords!

[16] Benjamin Disraeli, Earl of Beaconsfield, *Lord George Bentinck: A Political Biography* (London: Colburn and Co., 1852).

CHRONOLOGICAL TABLE

The Bible does not offer a dated chronology about historical persons or events. This is true in spite of numerous valuable genealogies and other chronological details that accompany some historical data, especially in connection with the rise and fall of the kings of Israel. Therefore in dealing with a timetable relating to a goodly part of the Old Testament history, we will do well in establishing *approximate dates* until we reach the 8th - 7th century B.C.

YEAR

Prior to 2000 B.C......... ......The Beginnings, Genesis 1:11.

2000 - 1600 B.C.............The Patriarchal Period, Genesis 12-50; Job.

1500 - 1250 B.C.............The Period of Exodus, Moses, The Pentateuch, Joshua.

1250 - 1050 B.C.............The Period of Judges, Judges, Ruth, I Samuel 1-7.

1050 - 932 B.C.............The Period of the United Kingdom, Saul, David, Solomon; I Samuel 8 - I Kings 11; I Chronicles 10 - II Chronicles 9.

932 - 586 B.C.............From the Division of the Kingdom to the fall of Jerusalem, I Kings 12 - II Kings 25; II Chronicles 10-36; many Psalms and the Pre-exilic Prophets:

Hosea	750 - 725 B.C.	
Joel	835 - 796 B.C.	
Amos	765 - 750 B.C.	
Obadiah	742 - 726 B.C.	Contemporaries of Isaiah.
Jonah	790 - 724 B.C.	
Isaiah	740 - 690 B.C.	
Micah	725 - 695 B.C.	

(Fall of Samaria — 721 B.C.)

Nahum	660 - 607 B.C.	From the end of the Assyrian invasion to the beginning of the Babylonian invasion.
Habakkuk	687 - 642 B.C.	
Zephaniah	630 - 610 B.C.	
Jeremiah	627 - 586 B.C.	

148

(Destruction of Jerusalem by
Nebuchadnezzar — 586 B.C.)

586 - 538 B.C................The Babylonian Exile, I and II Kings; Jeremiah, Lamentations.

Ezekiel	592 - 572 B.C.	
Daniel	603 - 534 B.C.	During and after the
Haggai	520 - 516 B.C.	Babylonian exile.
Zechariah	520 - 518 B.C.	
Malachi	450 - 397 B.C.	

538 - 333 B.C................The Persian Period.
333 - 168 B.C................The Greek Period.
168 - 63 B.C................The Maccabean Period.
63 B.C. - 70 A.D................The Roman Period.
6 - 4 B.C................THE BIRTH OF CHRIST.

GLOSSARY

This short glossary, with the accompanying explanations, may be useful to most of the non-Jewish readers. It is not intended to be of any assistance to those of the Jewish readers who know Hebrew and are acquainted with post-Biblical literature.

ABOTH. "Fathers." A Treatise of the Mishna, with no Gemara attached to it. It contains a large number of important ethical sayings and may be found in English translation in several of the Daily Prayer Books. It is also known as the sayings of the Fathers.

AMIDDAH, STANDING. Also known as the Shemoneh Esreh, the Eighteen Benedictions which form the basis of the Daily Service.

AMORITE. Israel's degeneracy is traced back to its origin in the Amorites and Hittites. In Joshua 10:5, 6 they are referred to as original inhabitants of Jerusalem, Hebron, etc. Recent discoveries indicate that as late as Rehoboam, Amorites prevailed in South Judea.

ASSYRIA. Assyria and Egypt are mentioned as the former cruel oppressors of Israel. They with Babylon had gone far beyond the purpose of the divine will in chastisement. They had given double what they should have given (Isa. 40:1; Jer. 46:28).

BIBLE. The Hebrew Bible is arranged under the following heads:
 I. Torah or The Law. The Five Books of Moses.
 II. Neviim, The Prophets: (1) Former Prophets, Joshua, Judges,

I and II Samuel, I and II Kings; (2) Latter Prophets, Isaiah, Jeremiah, Ezekiel, Daniel, and the Twelve Minor Prophets.

III. *Ketubim,* The Writings: (1) Psalms, Proverbs, Job; (2) The five Megilloth, Song of Songs, Ruth, Lamentations, Ecclesiastes, Esther; (3) Ezra and Nehemiah, I and II Chronicles. The Jews often speak of the Scriptures as Tanach.

BIRCATH HAMMINIM. A benediction or "malediction" against the heretics, was composed by Samuel the Younger about 100 A.D. at the request of Rabbi Gamaliel.

BREAD OF MOURNING. Peculiar customs attended funerals in the East. A feast followed them (Hos. 9:4).

CHALDEA. Isaiah had condemned intrigue and political alliance with Babylon in 710 B.C. (Isa. 39:1-8). Kaldu is the old name of the country, hence Kasdim in Hebrew from Kesed (Gen. 22:22). Thus from the early days Babylon had a prominent empire-power, though now and then overshadowed by Assyria.

EMUNAH. "The righteous shall live by his faith" (Hab. 2:4). In the Talmud (Makkot 23b), there is a famous remark of R. Simlai: "Moses gave Israel 613 commandments. David reduced them to 10, Isaiah to 2, but Habakkuk to one: 'The righteous shall live by his faith.' "

EPHRAIM. The leading Tribe among the Ten, is often used to denote the whole kingdom of Samaria.

HEBREW. Often spoken of as "Loshon Kodesh" because it was the language of the Bible. There have been five periods in the development of Hebrew: (1) the Biblical period; (2) the Talmudic period; (3) the Spanish period; (4) the Haskalah period, and (5) the Hebrew revival period of our day.

ISRAEL. Whole people of the twelve tribes. After the captivity the distinctive names, Ephraim and Judah, cease as the peoples are reunited.

JEHOVAH. The sacred name for the God of Israel. The Jews in reading the Hebrew use the word Adhonai, which means Lord. Sabaoth is rendered Hosts, Jehovah Sabaoth as Isaiah often uses Jehovah, as supreme sovereign over all.

JESHURUN. An endearing name for Israel. Derived perhaps from Jasher "the upright one" (Isa. 44:2).

MESSIAH BEN JOSEPH. The contradiction between the Jewish doctrine of the Messiah and the conception presented in such passages as Isaiah 53, has resolved in the creation of a doctrine of a Messiah, called the Son of Joseph, who is to precede the great Messiah, the

Son of David, and atone by suffering and death for the sins of the people.

MIDRASH. Plural Midrashim. Explanations of different books of the Scriptures, or old rabbinical commentaries.

TALMUD. Plural Talmudim, "learning," "teaching." A summary of the oral law (Torah She-Be-Al Peh) supplementing the Bible. It is in two parts: (1) The Mishna, "repetition," statement of the Law, a part of the Talmud; (2) The Gemara, "completion," which takes the form of a commentary on the Mishna.

TARGUM. Plural Targumim. Aramaic versions of various parts of the Bible, have played an essential role in Jewish life since early times. This is evidenced by a Talmudic passage which says: "One should read the weekly portion of the Torah (Books of Moses) twice: once in the original text and once with the Targum." There are several such paraphrases; Targum of Onkelos of the second century A.D., Targum Jerusalem I and Targum Jerusalem II of the seventh century A.D., *On the Prophets,* Targum Jonathan ben Uzziel. Its present form is of about the fifth century A.D.

BIBLIOGRAPHY

American-Jewish Translation of the Scriptures (Philadelphia).

American Standard Version of the Bible (New York: Thomas Nelson & Sons).

Authorized (King James) Version of the Bible (Cleveland: The World Publishing Company).

Baron, David, *Rays of Messiah's Glory* (London: Hodder & Stoughton, 1888).

————, *Visions and Prophecies of Zechariah* (London: Hebrew Christian Testimony, 1956 reprint).

Briggs, C. A., *Messianic Prophecy* (New York: Scribner's Sons, 1895).

Cohen, A., ed., *The Twelve Prophets* (London: Soncino Press).

Delitzsch, Franz, *Old Testament History of Redemption and Commentary on Isaiah.*

Edersheim, Alfred, *Prophecy and History in Relation to the Messiah* (New York: Randolph Company).

Hengstenberg, E.W., *Christology of the Old Testament* (Edinburgh: T. & T. Clark, 1854-1858 and Kregel Publications, 1956).

Hertz, Rabbi, *The Pentateuch* (London: Soncino Press).

Jocz, J., *The Jewish People and Jesus Christ* (London: S.P.G.K., 1949).

Kirkpatrick, A. F., *The Doctrine of the Prophets* (London: Macmillan Co.).

Klausner, Joseph, *The Messianic Idea in Israel* (New York: Macmillan Co., 1955).

Paterson, John, *The Goodly Fellowship of the Prophets* (New York: Scribner's Sons).

Reich, Max I., *The Messianic Hope of Israel* (Grand Rapids: Wm. B. Eerdmans Publishing Co.).

Saphir, Adolph, *Christ and Israel* (London: Marshall, Morgan and Scott).

Silver, Abba Hillel, *A History of Messianic Speculation in Israel* (New York: Macmillan Co., 1927).

The Targums, Onkelos and Jonathan on the Pentateuch. These translations are side by side with the text of the Old Testament in several editions.

Unger, Merrill F., *Introductory Guide to the Old Testament* (Grand Rapids: Zondervan Publishing House, 1951).

Yehoash, The Old Testament (Hebrew-Yiddish) (New York: Jewish Journal Edition, 1935-45).

INDEX

Philo, 72
Piper, 64
Plato, 138
Porphyry, 115
Prophet Like Moses, The, 21-23
Prophets, The, 140
  Their Immediate Aim, 141
  Their Ultimate Aim, 141-145
Protevangelium, 13, 14

Rambam, 89
Ruth, 19

Samuel, 53
Samuel, E. Bender, 44, 144
Saphir, Adolph, 132
Satan, 14, 15
Scofield, C. I., 67
Seed of Abraham, The, 16, 17
Sennacherib, 44, 80, 81
Shadrach, Meshach, Abednego, 118
Shalmanezer, 49
Shear-jashub, 74
Shem, 15
Simon, 128
Sin, 13, 16
Smith, George Adam, 85, 91
Solomon, 15, 19, 55, 59, 88

Southern Kingdom, 50
Spurgeon, 39
Staudlin, 87
Star and Sceptre of Jacob, The, 23-27
Stephen, 117, 145

Targum Jerusalem, 20
Targum Jonathan, 26, 56
Targum Mammonides, 26
Targum Onkelos, 20, 25, 72
Targum Rashi, 26, 56, 77, 86, 128, 132
Timon, 89

Umbreit, 87
Unger, Merrill F., 54

Webster, Daniel, 96
Williams, A. Lukyn, 67
Wilson, Robert Dick, 72, 73, 121
Wolfe, 42
Woman of Samaria, 22

Yalkut, 89, 90

Zechariah, 49, 125-133
Zephaniah, 97, 98
Zerubbabel, 61, 77, 125, 126